Lady Inger of Ostrat

Henrik Ibsen

Translated by Charles Archer

DODO PRESS

HENRIK IBSEN'S PROSE DRAMAS, VOL. III

LADY INGER OF OSTRAT, Translation by Charles Archer

LADY INGER OF OSTRAT (1855.)

CHARACTERS.

LADY INGER OTTISDAUGHTER ROMER, widow of High Steward Nils Gyldenlove.
ELINA GYLDENLOVE, her daughter.
NILS LYKKE, Danish knight and councilor.
OLAF SKAKTAVL, an outlawed Norwegian noble.
NILS STENSSON.
JENS BIELKE, Swedish commander.
BIORN, major-domo at Ostrat.
FINN, a servant.
EINAR HUK, bailiff at Ostrat.
Servants, peasants, and Swedish men-at-arms.

The action takes place at Ostrat Manor, on the Trondhiem Fiord, the year 1528.

[PRONUNCIATION of NAMES. —Ostrat=Ostrot; Inger=Ingher (g nearly as in "ringer"); Gyldenlove=Ghyldenlove; Elina (Norwegian, Eline)= Eleena; Stennson=Staynson; Biorn=Byorn; Jens Bielke=Yens Byelke; Huk=Hook. The final e's and the o's pronounced much as in German.]LADY INGER OF OSTRAT

DRAMA IN FIVE ACTS.

ACT FIRST.

(A room at Ostrat. Through an open door in the back, the Banquet Hall is seen in faint moonlight, which shines fitfully through a deep bow-window in the opposite wall. To the right, an entrance- door; further forward, a curtained window. On the left, a door leading to the inner rooms; further forward a large, open fireplace, which casts a glow over the room. It is a stormy evening.)

(BIORN and FINN are sitting by the fireplace. The latter is occupied in polishing a helmet. Several pieces of armour lie near them, along with a sword and shield.)

FINN (after a pause). Who was Knut* Alfson?

* Pronounce *Knoot*.

BIORN. My Lady says he was the last of Norway's knighthood.

FINN. And the Danes killed him at Oslo-fiord?

BIORN. Ask any child of five, if you know not that.

FINN. So Knut Alfson was the last of our knighthood? And now he's dead and gone! (Holds up the helmet.) Well then, hang thou scoured and bright in the Banquet Hall; for what art thou now but an empty nut-shell? The kernel—the worms have eaten that many a winter agone. What say you, Biorn—may not one call Norway's land an empty nut- shell, even like the helmet here; bright without, worm-eaten within?

BIORN. Hold your peace, and mind your work! —Is the helmet ready?

FINN. It shines like silver in the moonlight.

BIORN. Then put it by. —— —— See here; scrape the rust off the sword.

FINN (turning the sword over and examining it). Is it worth while?

BIORN. What mean you?

FINN. The edge is gone.

BIORN. What's that to you? Give it me. —— —— Here, take the shield.

FINN (as before). There's no grip to it!

BIORN (mutters). If once I got a grip on *you*——

(FINN hums to himself for a while.)

BIORN. What now?

FINN. An empty helmet, an edgeless sword, a shield without a grip—there's the whole glory for you. I see not that any can blame Lady Inger for leaving such weapons to hang scoured and polished on the walls, instead of rusting them in Danish blood.

BIORN. Folly! Is there not peace in the land?

FINN. Peace? Ay, when the peasant has shot away his last arrow, and the wolf has reft the last lamb from the fold, then is there peace between them. But 'tis a strange friendship. Well well; let that pass. It is fitting, as I said, that the harness hang bright in the hall; for you know the old saw: "Call none a man but the knightly man. " Now there is no knight left in our land; and where no man is, there must women order things; therefore— —

BIORN. Therefore—therefore I order you to hold your foul prate! (Rises.) It grows late. Go hang helm and harness in the hall again.

FINN (in a low voice). Nay, best let it be till tomorrow.

BIORN. What, do you fear the dark?

FINN. Not by day. And if so be I fear it at even, I am not the only one. Ah, you look; I tell you in the housefolk's room there is talk of many things. (Lower.) They say that night by night a tall figure, clad in black, walks the Banquet Hall.

BIORN. Old wives' tales!

FINN. Ah, but they all swear 'tis true.

BIORN. That I well believe.

FINN. The strangest of all is that Lady Inger thinks the same— —

BIORN (starting). Lady Inger? What does she think?

FINN. What Lady Inger thinks no one can tell. But sure it is that she has no rest in her. See you not how day by day she grows thinner and paler? (Looks keenly at him.) They say she never sleeps—and that it is because of the dark figure— —

(While he is speaking, ELINA GYLDENLOVE has appeared in the half-open door on the left. She stops and listens, unobserved.)

BIORN. And you believe such follies?

FINN. Well, half and half. There be folk, too, that read things another way. But that is pure malice, for sure. —Hearken, Biorn— know you the song that is going round the country?

BIORN. A song?

FINN. Ay, 'tis on all folks' lips. 'Tis a shameful scurril thing, for sure; yet it goes prettily. Just listen (sings in a low voice):

Dame Inger sitteth in Ostrat fair,
She wraps her in costly furs—
She decks her in velvet and ermine and vair,
Red gold are the beads that she twines in her hair—
But small peace in that soul of hers.

Dame Inger hath sold her to Denmark's lord.
She bringeth her folk 'neath the stranger's yoke—
In guerdon whereof— — — —

(BIORN enraged, seizes him by the throat. ELINA GYLDENLOVE withdraws without having been seen.)

BIORN. And I will send you guerdonless to the foul fiend, if you prate of Lady Inger but one unseemly word more.

FINN (breaking from his grasp). Why—did *I* make the song?

(The blast of a horn is heard from the right.)

BIORN. Hush—what is that?

FINN. A horn. So we are to have guests to-night.

BIORN (at the window). They are opening the gate. I hear the clatter of hoofs in the courtyard. It must be a knight.

FINN. A knight? A knight can it scarce be.

BIORN. Why not?

FINN. You said it yourself: the last of our knighthood is dead and gone. (Goes out to the right.)

BIORN. The accursed knave, with his prying and peering! What avails all my striving to hide and hush things? They whisper of her even now——; ere long will all men be clamouring for——

ELINA (comes in again through the door on the left; looks round her, and says with suppressed emotion). Are you alone, Biorn?

BIORN. Is it you, Mistress Elina?

ELINA. Come, Biorn, tell me one of your stories; I know you have more to tell than those that——

BIORN. A story? Now—so late in the evening——?

ELINA. If you count from the time when it grew dark at Ostrat, it is late indeed.

BIORN. What ails you? Has aught crossed you? You seem so restless.

ELINA. May be so.

BIORN. There is something the matter. I have hardly known you this half year past.

ELINA. Bethink you: this half year past my dearest sister Lucia has been sleeping in the vault below.

BIORN. That is not all, Mistress Elina—it is not that alone that makes you now thoughtful and white and silent, now restless and ill at ease, as you are to-night.

ELINA. You think so? And wherefore not? Was she not gentle and pure and fair as a summer night? Biorn, I tell you, Lucia was dear to me as my life. Have you forgotten how many a time, as children, we sat on your knee in the winter evenings? You sang songs to us, and told us tales——

BIORN. Ay, then your were blithe and gay.

ELINA. Ah, then, Biorn! Then I lived a glorious life in the fable-land of my own imaginings. Can it be that the sea-strand was naked then as now? If it were so, I did not know it. It was there I loved to go, weaving all my fair romances; my heroes came from afar and sailed again across the sea; I lived in their midst, and set forth with them when they sailed away. (Sinks on a chair.) Now I feel so faint and weary; I can live no longer in my tales. They are only—tales. (Rises hastily.) Biorn, do you know what has made me sick? A truth; a hateful, hateful truth, that gnaws me day and night.

BIORN. What mean you?

ELINA. Do you remember how sometimes you would give us good counsel and wise saws? Sister Lucia followed them; but I—ah, well-a-day!

BIORN (consoling her). Well, well— —!

ELINA. I know it—I was proud and self-centred! In all our games, I would still be the Queen, because I was the tallest, the fairest, the wisest! I know it!

BIORN. That is true.

ELINA. Once you took me by the hand and looked earnestly at me, and said: "Be not proud of your fairness, or your wisdom; but be proud as the mountain eagle as often as you think: I am Inger Gyldenlove's daughter! "

BIORN. And was it not matter enough for pride?

ELINA. You told me so often enough, Biorn! Oh, you told me so many tales in those days. (Presses his hand.) Thanks for them all! Now, tell me one more; it might make me light of heart again, as of old.

BIORN. You are a child no longer.

ELINA. Nay, indeed! But let me dream that I am. —Come, tell on!

(Throws herself into a chair. BIORN sits in the chimney-corner.)

BIORN. Once upon a time there was a high-born knight— —

ELINA (who has been listening restlessly in the direction of the hall, seizes his arm and breaks out in a vehement whisper). Hush! No need to shout so loud; I can hear well!

BIORN (more softly). Once upon a time there was a high-born knight, of whom there went the strange report— —

(ELINA half-rises and listens in anxious suspense in the direction of the hall.)

BIORN. Mistress Elina, what ails you?

ELINA (sits down again). Me? Nothing. Go on.

BIORN. Well, as I was saying, when he did but look straight in a woman's eyes, never could she forget it after; her thoughts must follow him wherever he went, and she must waste away with sorrow.

ELINA. I have heard that tale— — — — And, moreover, 'tis no tale you are telling, for the knight you speak of is Nils Lykke, who sits even now in the Council of Denmark— —

BIORN. May be so.

ELINA. Well, let it pass—go on!

BIORN. Now it happened once— —

ELINA (rises suddenly). Hush; be still!

BIORN. What now? What is the matter?

ELINA. It *is* there! Yes, by the cross of Christ it *is* there!

BIORN (rises). What is there? Where?

ELINA. It is she—in the hall. (Goes hastily towards the hall.)

BIORN (following). How can you think— —? Mistress Elina, go to your chamber!

ELINA. Hush; stand still! Do not move; do not let her see you! Wait—the moon is coming out. Can you not see the black-robed figure——?

BIORN. By all the holy——!

ELINA. Do you see—she turns Knut Alfson's picture to the wall. Ha-ha; be sure it looks her too straight in the eyes!

BIORN. Mistress Elina, hear me!

ELINA (going back towards the fireplace). Now I know what I know!

BIORN (to himself). Then it is true!

ELINA. Who was it, Biorn? Who was it?

BIORN. You saw as plainly as I.

ELINA. Well? Whom did I see?

BIORN. You saw your mother.

ELINA (half to herself). Night after night I have heard her steps in there. I have heard her whispering and moaning like a soul in pain. And what says the song—— Ah, now I know! Now I know that——

BIORN. Hush!

(LADY INGER GYLDENLOVE enters rapidly from the hall, without noticing the others; she goes to the window, draws the curtain, and gazes out as if watching for some one on the high road; after a while, she turns and goes slowly back into the hall.)

ELINA (softly, following her with her eyes). White as a corpse——!

(An uproar of many voices is heard outside the door on the right.)

BIORN. What can this be?

ELINA. Go out and see what is amiss.

(EINAR HUK, the bailiff, appears in the ante-room, with a crowd of Retainers and Peasants.)

EINAR HUK (in the doorway). Straight in to her! And see you lose not heart!

BIORN. What do you seek?

EINAR HUK. Lady Inger herself.

BIORN. Lady Inger? So late?

EINAR HUK. Late, but time enough, I wot.

THE PEASANTS. Yes, yes; she must hear us now!

(The whole rabble crowds into the room. At the same moment, LADY INGER appears in the doorway of the hall. A sudden silence.)

LADY INGER. What would you with me?

EINAR HUK. We sought you, noble lady, to— —

LADY INGER. Well, speak out!

EINAR HUK. Why, we are not ashamed of our errand. In one word, we come to pray you for weapons and leave— —

LADY INGER. Weapons and leave— —? And for what?

EINAR HUK. There has come a rumour from Sweden that the people of the Dales have risen against King Gustav— —

LADY INGER. The people of the Dales?

EINAR HUK. Ay, so the tidings run, and they seem sure enough.

LADY INGER. Well, if it were so, what have you to do with the Dale-folk's rising?

THE PEASANTS. We will join them! We will help! We will free ourselves!

LADY INGER (aside). Can the time be come?

EINAR HUK. From all our borderlands the peasants are pouring across to the Dales. Even outlaws that have wandered for years in the mountains are venturing down to the homesteads again, and drawing men together, and whetting their rusty swords.

LADY INGER (after a pause). Tell me, men, have you thought well of this? Have you counted the cost, if King Gustav's men should win?

BIORN (softly and imploringly to LADY INGER). Count the cost to the Danes if King Gustav's men should lose.

LADY INGER (evasively). That reckoning is not for me to make. (Turns to the people). You know that King Gustav is sure of help from Denmark. King Frederick is his friend, and will never leave him in the lurch——

EINAR HUK. But if the people were now to rise all over Norway's land? —if we all rose as one man, nobles and peasants together? —ay, Lady Inger Gyldenlove, the time we have waited for is surely come. We have but to rise now to drive the strangers from the land.

THE PEASANTS. Ay, out with the Danish sheriffs! Out with the foreign masters! Out with the Councillors' lackeys!

LADY INGER (aside). Ah, there is metal in them; and yet, yet——!

BIORN (to himself). She is of two minds. (To ELINA.) What say you now, Mistress Elina—have you not sinned in misjudging your mother?

ELINA. Biorn, if my eyes have deceived me, I could tear them out of my head!

EINAR HUK. See you not, my noble lady, King Gustav must be dealt with first. Once his power is gone, the Danes cannot long hold this land——

LADY INGER. And then?

EINAR HUK. Then we shall be free. We shall have no more foreign masters, and can choose ourselves a king, as the Swedes have done before us.

LADY INGER (with animation). A king for ourselves. Are you thinking of the Sture stock?

EINAR HUK. King Christiern and others after him have swept bare our ancient houses. The best of our nobles are outlaws on the hill-paths, if so be they still live; nevertheless, it might still be possible to find one or other shoot of the old stems— —

LADY INGER (hastily). Enough, Einar Huk, enough! (To herself.) Ah, my dearest hope! (Turns to the Peasants and Retainers.) I have warned you, now, as well as I can. I have told you how great is the risk you run. But if you are fixed in your purpose, it were folly of me to forbid what I have no power to prevent.

EINAR HUK. Then we have your leave to— —?

LADY INGER. You have your own firm will; take counsel with that. If it be as you say, that you are daily harassed and oppressed— — — — I know but little of these matters, and would not know more. What can I, a lonely woman— —? Even if you were to plunder the Banquet Hall—and there's many a good weapon on the walls—you are the masters at Ostrat to-night. You must do as seems good to you. Good-night!

(Loud cries of joy from the multitude. Candles are lighted; the retainers bring weapons of different kinds from the hall.)

BIORN (seizes LADY INGER'S hand as she is going). Thanks, my noble and high-souled mistress! I, that have known you from childhood up—I have never doubted you.

LADY INGER. Hush, Biorn. It is a dangerous game that I have ventured this night. The others stake only their lives; but I, trust me, a thousandfold more!

BIORN. How mean you? Do you fear for your power and your favour with— —?

LADY INGER. My power? O God in Heaven!

A RETAINER (comes from the hall with a large sword). See, here's a real good wolf's-tooth to flay the blood-suckers' lackeys with!

EINAR HUK. 'Tis too good for such as you. Look, here is the shaft of Sten Sture's* lance; hang the breastplate upon it, and we shall have the noblest standard heart can desire.

* Pronounce *Stayn Stoore* [umlaut above "e"—D. L.].

FINN (comes from the door on the left, with a letter in his hand, and goes towards LADY INGER). I have sought you through all the house.

LADY INGER. What do you want?

FINN (hands her the letter). A messenger is come from Trondhiem with a letter for you.

LADY INGER. Let me see! (opening the letter). From Trondhiem? What can it be? (Runs through the letter.) Help, Christ! From him! and here in Norway——

(Reads on with strong emotion, while the men go on bringing out arms from the hall.)

LADY INGER (to herself). He is coming here. He is coming to- night! —Ay, then 'tis with our wits we must fight, not with the sword.

EINAR HUK. Enough, enough, good fellows; we are well armed now, and can set forth on our way.

LADY INGER (with a sudden change of tone). No man shall leave my house to-night!

EINAR HUK. But the wind is fair, noble lady; we can sail up the fiord, and——

LADY INGER. It shall be as I have said.

EINAR HUK. Are we to wait till to-morrow, then?

LADY INGER. Till to-morrow, and longer still. No armed man shall go forth from Ostrat yet awhile.

(Signs of displeasure from the crowd.)

SOME OF THE PEASANTS. We will go all the same, Lady Inger!

THE CRY SPREADS. Yes, yes; we *will* go!

LADY INGER (advancing a step towards them). Who dares to move? (A silence. After a moment's pause, she adds:) I have thought for you. What do you common folk know of the country's needs? How dare you judge of such things? You must even bear your oppressions and burdens yet awhile. Why murmur at that, when you see that we, your leaders, are as ill bested as you? —— —— Take all the weapons back to the hall. You shall know my further will hereafter. Go!

(The Retainers take back the arms, and the whole crowd then withdraws by the door on the right.)

ELINA (softly to BIORN). Do you still think I have sinned in misjudging—the Lady of Ostrat?

LADY INGER (beckons to BIORN, and says). Have a guest chamber ready.

BIORN. It is well, Lady Inger!

LADY INGER. And let the gate stand open to all that knock.

BIORN. But——?

LADY INGER. The gate open!

BIORN. The gate open. (Goes out to the right.)

LADY INGER (to ELINA, who has already reached the door on the left). Stay here! —— —— Elina—my child—I have something to say to you alone.

ELINA. I hear you.

LADY INGER. Elina—— ——you think evil of your mother.

ELINA. I think, to my sorrow, what your deeds have forced me to think.

LADY INGER. You answer out of the bitterness of your heart.

ELINA. Who has filled my heart with bitterness? From my childhood I have been wont to look up to you as a great and high-souled woman. It was in your likeness I pictured the women we read of in the chronicles and the Book of Heroes. I thought the Lord God himself had set his seal on your brow, and marked you out as the leader of the helpless and the oppressed. Knights and nobles sang your praise in the feast-hall, and the peasants, far and near, called you the country's pillar and its hope. All thought that through you the good times were to come again! All thought that through you a new day was to dawn over the land! The night is still here; and I no longer know if I dare look for any morning to come through you.

LADY INGER. It is easy to see whence you have learnt such venomous words. You have let yourself give ear to what the thoughtless rabble mutters and murmurs about things it can little judge of.

ELINA. "Truth is in the people's mouth, " was your word when they praised you in speech and song.

LADY INGER. May be so. But if indeed I had chosen to sit here idle, though it was my part to act—do you not think that such a choice were burden enough for me, without your adding to its weight?

ELINA. The weight I add to your burden bears on me as heavily as on you. Lightly and freely I drew the breath of life, so long as I had you to believe in. For my pride is my life; and well had it become me, if you had remained what once you were.

LADY INGER. And what proves to you I have not? Elina, how can you know so surely that you are not doing your mother wrong?

ELINA (vehemently). Oh, that I were!

LADY INGER. Peace! You have no right to call your mother to account—— With a single word I could—— ——; but it would be an ill word for you to hear; you must await what time shall bring; may be that——

ELINA (turns to go). Sleep well, my mother!

LADY INGER (hesitates). Nay, stay with me; I have still somewhat— Come nearer; —you must hear me, Elina!

(Sits down by the table in front of the window.)

ELINA. I am listening.

LADY INGER. For as silent as you are, I know well that you often long to be gone from here. Ostrat is too lonely and lifeless for you.

ELINA. Do you wonder at that, my mother?

LADY INGER. It rests with you whether all this shall henceforth be changed.

ELINA. How so?

LADY INGER. Listen. —I look for a guest to-night.

ELINA (comes nearer). A guest?

LADY INGER. A stranger, who must remain a stranger to all. None must know whence he comes or whither he goes.

ELINA (throws herself, with a cry of joy, at her mother's feet and seizes her hands). My mother! My mother! Forgive me, if you can, all the wrong I have done you!

LADY INGER. What do you mean? Elina, I do not understand you.

ELINA. Then they were all deceived! You are still true at heart!

LADY INGER. Rise, rise and tell me——

ELINA. Do you think I do not know who the stranger is?

LADY INGER. You know? And yet——?

ELINA. Do you think the gates of Ostrat shut so close that never a whisper of evil tidings can slip through? Do you think I do not know that the heir of many a noble line wanders outlawed, without rest or shelter, while Danish masters lord it in the home of their fathers?

LADY INGER. And what then?

ELINA. I know well that many a high-born knight is hunted through the woods like a hungry wolf. No hearth has he to rest by, no bread to eat— —

LADY INGER (coldly). Enough! Now I understand you.

ELINA (continuing). And that is why the gates of Ostrat must stand open by night! That is why he must remain a stranger to all, this guest of whom none must know whence he comes or whither he goes! You are setting at naught the harsh decree that forbids you to harbour or succor the exiles— —

LADY INGER. Enough, I say! (After a short silence, adds with an effort:) You mistake, Elina—it is no outlaw that I look for— —

ELINA (rises). Then I have understood you ill indeed.

LADY INGER. Listen to me, my child; but think as you listen; if indeed you can tame that wild spirit of yours.

ELINA. I am tame, till you have spoken.

LADY INGER. Then hear what I have to say—I have sought, so far as lay in my power, to keep you in ignorance of all our griefs and miseries. What could it avail to fill your young heart with wrath and care? It is not weeping and wailing of women that can free us from our evil lot; we need the courage and strength of men.

ELINA. Who has told you that, when courage and strength are indeed needed, I shall be found wanting?

LADY INGER. Hush, child; —I might take you at your word.

ELINA. How mean you, my mother?

LADY INGER. I might call on you for both; I might— —; but let me say my say out first. Know then that the time seems now to be drawing nigh, towards which the Danish Council have been working for many a year—the time for them to strike a final blow at our rights and our freedom. Therefore must we now——

ELINA (eagerly). Throw off the yoke, my mother?

LADY INGER. No; we must gain breathing-time. The Council is now sitting in Copenhagen, considering how best to aim the blow. Most of them are said to hold that there can be no end to dissensions till Norway and Denmark are one; for if we should still have our rights as a free land when the time comes to choose the next king, it is most like that the feud will break out openly. Now the Danish Councillors would hinder this——

ELINA. Ay, they would hinder it——! But are we to endure such things? Are we to look on quietly while——?

LADY INGER. No, we will not endure it. But to take up arms—to begin open warfare—what would come of that, so long as we are not united? And were we ever less united in this land than we are even now? —No, if aught is to be done, it must be done secretly and in silence. Even as I said, we must have time to draw breath. In the South, a good part of the nobles are for the Dane; but here in the North they are still in doubt. Therefore King Frederick has sent hither one of his most trusted councillors, to assure himself with his own eyes how we stand affected.

ELINA (anxiously). Well—and then——?

LADY INGER. He is the guest I look for to-night.

ELINA. He comes here? And to-night?

LADY INGER. He reached Trondhiem yesterday by a trading ship. Word has just been brought that he is coming to visit me; he may be here within the hour.

ELINA. Have you not thought, my mother, how it will endanger your fame thus to receive the Danish envoy? Do not the people already regard you with distrustful eyes? How can you hope that, when the time comes, they will let you rule and guide them, if it be known——

LADY INGER. Fear not. All this I have fully weighed; but there is no danger. His errand in Norway is a secret; he has come unknown to Trondhiem, and unknown shall he be our guest at Ostrat.

ELINA. And the name of this Danish lord——?

LADY INGER. It sounds well, Elina; Denmark has scarce a nobler name.

ELINA. But what do you propose then? I cannot yet grasp your meaning.

LADY INGER. You will soon understand. —Since we cannot trample on the serpent, we must bind him.

ELINA. Take heed that he burst not your bonds.

LADY INGER. It rests with you to tighten them as you will.

ELINA. With me?

LADY INGER. I have long seen that Ostrat is as a cage to you. The young falcon chafes behind the iron bars.

ELINA. My wings are clipped. Even if you set me free—it would avail me little.

LADY INGER. Your wings are not clipped, except by your own will.

ELINA. Will? My will is in your hands. Be what you once were, and I too——

LADY INGER. Enough, enough. Hear what remains—— It would scarce break your heart to leave Ostrat?

ELINA. Maybe not, my mother!

LADY INGER. You told me once, that you lived your happiest life in tales and histories. What if that life were to be yours once more?

ELINA. What mean you?

LADY INGER. Elina—if a mighty noble were now to come and lead you to his castle, where you should find damsels and pages, silken robes and lofty halls awaiting you?

ELINA. A noble, you say?

LADY INGER. A noble.

ELINA (more softly). And the Danish envoy comes here to-night?

LADY INGER. To-night.

ELINA. If so be, then I fear to read the meaning of your words.

LADY INGER. There is nought to fear if you misread them not. Be sure it is far from my thought to put force upon you. You shall choose for yourself in this matter, and follow your own counsel.

ELINA (comes a step nearer). Have you heard the story of the mother that drove across the hills by night with her little children by her in the sledge? The wolves were on her track; it was life or death with her; —and one by one she cast out her little ones, to gain time and save herself.

LADY INGER. Nursery tales! A mother would tear the heart from her breast, before she would cast her child to the wolves!

ELINA. Were I not my mother's daughter, I would say you were right. But you are like that mother; one by one you have cast out your daughters to the wolves. The eldest went first. Five years ago Merete* went forth from Ostrat; now she dwells in Bergen and is Vinzents Lunge's** wife. But think you she is happy as the Danish noble's lady? Vinzents Lunge is mighty, well-nigh as a king; Merete has damsels and pages, silken robes and lofty halls; but the day has no sunshine for her, and the night no rest; for she has never loved him. He came hither and he wooed her; for she was the greatest heiress in Norway, and he needed to gain a footing in the land. I know it; I know it well! Merete bowed to your will; she went with the stranger lord. —But what has it cost her? More tears than a mother should wish to answer for at the day of reckoning.

* Pronounce *Mayrayte* ** Pronounce *Loonghe*.

LADY INGER. I know my reckoning, and I fear it not.

ELINA. Your reckoning ends not here. Where is Lucia, your second child?

LADY INGER. Ask God, who took her.

ELINA. It is you I ask; it is you that must answer for her young life. She was glad as a bird in spring when she sailed from Ostrat to be Merete's guest. A year passed, and she stood in this room once more; but her cheeks were white, and death had gnawed deep into her breast. Ah, you wonder at me, my mother! You thought that the ugly secret was buried with her; —but she told me all. A courtly knight had won her heart. He would have wedded her. You knew that her honour was at stake; yet your will never bent—and your child had to die. You see, I know all!

LADY INGER. All? Then she told you his name?

ELINA. His name? No; his name she did not tell me. His name was a torturing horror to her; —she never uttered it.

LADY INGER (relieved, to herself). Ah, then you do *not* know all— — —— Elina—it is true that the whole of this matter was well known to me. But there is one thing about it you seem not to have noted. The lord whom Lucia met in Bergen was a Dane— —

ELINA. That too I know.

LADY INGER. And his love was a lie. With guile and soft speeches he had ensnared her.

ELINA. I know it; but nevertheless she loved him; and had you had a mother's heart, your daughter's honour had been more to you than all.

LADY INGER. Not more than her happiness. Do you think that, with Merete's lot before my eyes, I could sacrifice my second child to a man that loved her not?

ELINA. Cunning words may befool many, but they befool not me— — Think not I know nothing of all that is passing in our land. I understand your counsels but too well. I know well that our Danish lords have no true friend in you. It may be that you hate them; but your fear them too. When you gave Merete to Vinzents Lunge the Danes held the mastery on all sides throughout our land. Three years later, when you forbade Lucia to wed the man she had given her life to, though he had deceived her, —things were far different then. The King's Danish governors had shamefully misused the common people, and you thought it not wise to link yourself still more closely to the foreign tyrants. And what have you done to avenge her that had to die so young? You have done nothing. Well then, I will act in your stead; I will avenge all the shame they have brought upon our people and our house.

LADY INGER. You? What will you do?

ELINA. I shall go *my* way, even as you go yours. What I shall do I myself know not; but I feel within me the strength to dare all for our righteous cause.

LADY INGER. Then you have a hard fight before you. I once promised as you do now—and my hair has grown grey under the burden of that promise.

ELINA. Good-night! Your guest will soon be here, and at that meeting I should be out of place. It may be there is yet time for you—— ——; well, God strengthen you and guide your way! Forget not that the eyes of many thousands are fixed upon you. Think on Merete, weeping late and early over her wasted life. Think on Lucia, sleeping in her black coffin. And one thing more. Forget not that in the game you play this night, your stake is your last child.

(Goes out to the left.)

LADY INGER (looks after her awhile). My last child? You know not how true was that word—— —— But the stake is not my child only. God help me, I am playing to-night for the whole of Norway's land. Ah—is not that some one riding through the gateway? (Listens at the window.) No; not yet. Only the wind; it blows cold as the grave—— —— Has God a right to do this? —To make me a woman—and then to lay a man's duty upon my shoulders? For I *have* the welfare of the country in my hands. It *is* in my power to make them rise as one man. They look to *me* for the signal; and if I give it not now—— it may never be given. To delay? To sacrifice the many for the sake of one? —Were it not better if I could—— ——? No, no, no—I *will* not! I *cannot!* (Steals a glance towards the Banquet Hall, but turns away again as if in dread, and whispers:) I can see them in there now. Pale spectres—dead ancestors— fallen kinsfolk. —Ah, those eyes that pierce me from every corner! (Makes a backward gesture with her hand, and cries:) Sten Sture! Knut Alfson! Olaf Skaktavl! Back—back! —I *cannot* do this!

(A STRANGER, strongly built, and with grizzled hair and beard, has entered from the Banquet Hall. He is dressed in a torn lambskin tunic; his weapons are rusty.)

THE STRANGER (stops in the doorway, and says in a low voice). Hail to you, Inger Gyldenlove!

LADY INGER (turns with a scream). Ah, Christ in heaven save me!

(Falls back into a chair. The STRANGER stands gazing at her, motionless, leaning on his sword.)

ACT SECOND.

(The room at Ostrat, as in the first Act.)

(LADY INGER GYLDENLOVE is seated at the table on the right, by the window. OLAF SKAKTAVL is standing a little way from her. Their faces show that they have been engaged in an animated discussion.)

OLAF SKAKTAVL. For the last time, Inger Gyldenlove—you are not to be moved from your purpose?

LADY INGER. I can do nought else. And my counsel to you is: do as I do. If it be heaven's will that Norway perish utterly, perish it must, for all we may do to save it.

OLAF SKAKTAVL. And think you I can content myself with words like these? Shall I sit and look quietly on, now that the hour is come? Do you forget the reckoning I have to pay? They have robbed me of my lands, and parcelled them out among themselves. My son, my only child, the last of my race, they have slaughtered like a dog. Myself they have outlawed and forced to lurk by forest and fell these twenty years. —Once and again have folk whispered of my death; but this I believe, that they shall not lay me beneath the earth before I have seen my vengeance.

LADY INGER. Then is there a long life before you. What would you do?

OLAF SKAKTAVL. Do? How should I know what I will do? It has never been my part to plot and plan. That is where you must help me. You have the wit for that. I have but my sword and my two arms.

LADY INGER. Your sword is rusted, Olaf Skaktavl! All the swords in Norway are rusted.

OLAF SKAKTAVL. That is doubtless why some folk fight only with their tongues. —Inger Gyldenlove—great is the change in you. Time was when the heart of a man beat in your breast.

LADY INGER. Put me not in mind of what was.

OLAF SKAKTAVL. 'Tis for that alone I am here. You *shall* hear me, even if— —

LADY INGER. Be it so then; but be brief; for—I must say it— this is no place of safety for you.

OLAF SKAKTAVL. Ostrat is no place of safety for an outlaw? That I have long known. But you forget that an outlaw is unsafe wheresoever he may wander.

LADY INGER. Speak then; I will not hinder you.

OLAF SKAKTAVL. It is nigh on thirty years now since first I saw you. It was at Akershus* in the house of Knut Alfson and his wife. You were scarce more than a child then; yet you were bold as the soaring falcon, and wild and headstrong too at times. Many were the wooers around you. I too held you dear—dear as no woman before or since. But you cared for nothing, thought of nothing, save your country's evil case and its great need.

* Pronounce *Ahkers-hoos*.

LADY INGER. I counted but fifteen summers then—remember that. And was it not as though a frenzy had seized us all in those days?

OLAF SKAKTAVL. Call it what you will; but one thing I know—even the old and sober men among us doubted not that it was written in the counsels of the Lord that you were she who should break our thraldom and win us all our rights again. And more: you yourself then thought as we did.

LADY INGER. It was a sinful thought, Olaf Skaktavl. It was my proud heart, and not the Lord's call, that spoke in me.

OLAF SKAKTAVL. You could have been the chosen one had you but willed it. You came of the noblest blood in Norway; power and riches were at your feet; and you had an ear for the cries of anguish—then! — — — — Do you remember that afternoon when Henrik Krummedike and the Danish fleet anchored off Akershus? The captains of the fleet offered terms of settlement, and, trusting to the safe-conduct, Knut Alfson rowed on board. Three hours later, we bore him through the castle gate— —

LADY INGER. A corpse; a corpse!

OLAF SKAKTAVL. The best heart in Norway burst, when Krummedike's hirelings struck him down. Methinks I still can see the long procession that passed into the banquet-hall, heavily, two by two. There he lay on his bier, white as a spring cloud, with the axe- cleft in his brow. I may safely say that the boldest men in Norway were gathered there that night. Lady Margrete stood by her dead husband's head, and we swore as one man to venture lands and life to avenge this last misdeed and all that had gone before. — Inger Gyldenlove, —who was it that burst through the circle of men? A maiden—then almost a child—with fire in her eyes and her voice half choked with tears. — What was it she swore? Shall I repeat your words?

LADY INGER. And how did the others keep their promise? I speak not of you, Olaf Skaktavl, but of your friends, all our Norwegian nobles? Not one of them, in all these years, has had the courage to be a man; and yet they lay it to my charge that I am a woman.

OLAF SKAKTAVL. I know what you would say. Why have they bent to the yoke, and not defied the tyrants to the last? 'Tis but too true; there is base metal enough in our noble houses nowadays. But had they held together—who knows what might have been? And you could have held them together, for before you all had bowed.

LADY INGER. My answer were easy enough, but it would scarce content you. So let us leave speaking of what cannot be changed. Tell me rather what has brought you to Ostrat. Do you need harbour? Well, I will try to hide you. If you would have aught else, speak out; you shall find me ready— —

OLAF SKAKTAVL. For twenty years have I been homeless. In the mountains of Jaemteland my hair has grown grey. My dwelling has been with wolves and bears. —You see, Lady Inger—*I* need you not; but both nobles and people stand in sore need of you.

LADY INGER. The old burden.

OLAF SKAKTAVL. Ay, it sounds but ill in your ears, I know; yet hear it you must for all that. In brief, then: I come from Sweden: troubles are at hand: the Dales are ready to rise.

LADY INGER. I know it.

OLAF SKAKTAVL. Peter Kanzler is with us—secretly, you understand.

LADY INGER (starting). Peter Kanzler?

OLAF SKAKTAVL. It is he that has sent me to Ostrat.

LADY INGER (rises). Peter Kanzler, say you?

OLAF SKAKTAVL. He himself; —but mayhap you no longer know him?

LADY INGER (half to herself). Only too well! —But tell me, I pray you, —what message do you bring?

OLAF SKAKTAVL. When the rumour of the rising reached the border mountains, where I then was, I set off at once into Sweden. 'Twas not hard to guess that Peter Kanzler had a finger in the game. I sought him out and offered to stand by him; —he knew me of old, as you know, and knew that he could trust me; so he has sent me hither.

LADY INGER (impatiently). Yes yes, —he sent you hither to——?

OLAF SKAKTAVL (with secrecy). Lady Inger—a stranger comes to Ostrat to-night.

LADY INGER (surprised). What? Know you that——?

OLAF SKAKTAVL. Assuredly I know it. I know all. 'Twas to meet him that Peter Kanzler sent me hither.

LADY INGER. To meet him? Impossible, Olaf Skaktavl, —impossible!

OLAF SKAKTAVL. 'Tis as I tell you. If he be not already come, he will soon——

LADY INGER. Yes, I know; but——

OLAF SKAKTAVL. Then you know of his coming?

LADY INGER. Ay, surely. He sent me a message. That was why they opened to you as soon as you knocked.

OLAF SKAKTAVL (listens). Hush! —some one is riding along the road. (Goes to the window.) They are opening the gate.

LADY INGER (looks out). It is a knight and his attendant. They are dismounting in the courtyard.

OLAF SKAKTAVL. Then it is he. His name?

LADY INGER. You know not his name?

OLAF SKAKTAVL. Peter Kanzler refused to tell it me. He would only say that I should find him at Ostrat the third evening after Martinmas— —

LADY INGER. Ay; even to-night.

OLAF SKAKTAVL. He was to bring letters with him, and from them, and from you, I was to learn who he is.

LADY INGER. Then let me lead you to your chamber. You have need of rest and refreshment. You shall soon have speech with the stranger.

OLAF SKAKTAVL. Well, be it as you will. (Both go out to the left.)

(After a short pause, FINN enters cautiously through the door on the right, looks round the room, and peeps into the Banquet Hall; he then goes back to the door, and makes a sign to some one outside. Immediately after, enter COUNCILLOR NILS LYKKE and the Swedish Commander, JENS BIELKE.)

NILS LYKKE (softly). No one?

FINN (in the same tone). No one, master!

NILS LYKKE. And we may depend on you in all things?

FINN. The commandant in Trondhiem has ever given me a name for trustiness.

NILS LYKKE. It is well; he has said as much to me. First of all, then—has there come any stranger to Ostrat to-night, before us?

FINN. Ay; a stranger came an hour since.

NILS LYKKE (softly, to JENS BIELKE). He is here. (Turns again to FINN.) Would you know him again? Have you seen him?

FINN. Nay, none have seen him, that I know, but the gatekeeper. He was brought at once to Lady Inger, and she— —

NILS LYKKE. Well? What of her? He is not gone again already?

FINN. No; but it seems she keeps him hidden in one of her own rooms; for— —

NILS LYKKE. It is well.

JENS BIELKE (whispers). Then the first thing is to put a guard on the gate; then we are sure of him.

NILS LYKKE (with a smile). Hm! (To FINN.) Tell me—is there any way of leaving the castle but by the gate? Gape not at me so! I mean—can one escape from Ostrat unseen, while the castle gate is shut?

FINN. Nay, that I know not. 'Tis true they talk of secret ways in the vaults beneath; but no one knows them save Lady Inger—and mayhap Mistress Elina.

JENS BIELKE. The devil!

NILS LYKKE. It is well. You may go.

FINN. And should you need me in aught again, you have but to open the second door on the right in the Banquet Hall, and I shall presently be at hand.

NILS LYKKE. Good. (Points to the entrance-door. FINN goes out.)

JENS BIELKE. Now, by my soul, dear friend and brother—this campaign is like to end but scurvily for both of us.

NILS LYKKE (with a smile). Oh—not for me, I hope.

JENS BIELKE. Not? First of all, there is small honour to be got in hunting an overgrown whelp like this Nils Sture. Are we to think him mad or in his sober senses after the pranks he has played? First he breeds bad blood among the peasants; promises them help and all their hearts can desire; —and then, when it comes to the pinch, off he runs to hide behind a petticoat! Moreover, to tell the truth, I repent that I followed your counsel and went not my own way.

NILS LYKKE (aside). Your repentance comes somewhat late, my brother.

JENS BIELKE. Look you, I have never loved digging at a badger's earth. I look for quite other sport. Here have I ridden all the way from the Jaemteland with my horsemen, and have got me a warrant from the Trondhiem commandant to search for the rebel wheresoever I please. All his tracks point towards Ostrat— —

NILS LYKKE. He *is* here! He *is* here, I tell you!

JENS BIELKE. If that were so, should we not have found the gate barred and well guarded? Would that we had; then could I have found use for my men-at-arms— —

NILS LYKKE. But instead, the gate is opened for us in hospitality. Mark now—if Inger Gyldenlove's fame belie her not, I warrant she will not let her guests lack for either meat or drink.

JENS BIELKE. Ay, to turn us aside from our errand! And what wild whim was that of yours to persuade me to leave my horsemen a good mile from the castle? Had we come in force— —

NILS LYKKE. She had made us none the less welcome for that. But mark well that then our coming had made a stir. The peasants round about had held it for an outrage against Lady Inger; she had risen high in their favour once more—and with that, look you, we were ill served.

JENS BIELKE. May be so. But what am I to do now? Count Sture is in Ostrat, you say. Ay, but how does that profit me? Be sure Lady Inger Gyldenlove has as many hiding-places as the fox, and more than one outlet to them. We two can go snuffing about here alone as long as we please. I would the devil had the whole affair!

NILS LYKKE. Well, then, my friend—if you like not the turn your errand has taken, you have but to leave the field to me.

JENS BIELKE. To you? What will you do?

NILS LYKKE. Caution and cunning may here do more than could be achieved by force of arms. —And to say truth, Captain Jens Bielke—something of the sort has been in my mind ever since we met in Trondhiem yesterday.

JENS BIELKE. Was that why you persuaded me to leave the men at arms?

NILS LYKKE. Both your purpose at Ostrat and mine could best be served without them; and so——

JENS BIELKE. The foul fiend seize you—I had almost said! And me to boot! Might I not have known that there is guile in all your dealings?

NILS LYKKE. Be sure I shall need all my guile here, if I am to face my foe with even weapons. And let me tell you 'tis of the utmost moment to me that I acquit me of my mission secretly and well. You must know that when I set forth I was scarce in favour with my lord the King. He held me in suspicion; though I dare swear I have served him as well as any man could, in more than one ticklish charge.

JENS BIELKE. That you may safely boast. God and all men know you for the craftiest devil in all the three kingdoms.

NILS LYKKE. You flatter! But after all, 'tis not much to say. Now this present errand I hold for the crowning proof of my policy; for here I have to outwit a woman——

JENS BIELKE. Ha-ha-ha! In that art you have long since given crowning proofs of your skill, dear brother. Think you we in Sweden know not the song—

Fair maidens a-many they sigh and they pine;
"Ah God, that Nils Lykke were mine, mine, mine!"

NILS LYKKE. Alas, it is women of twenty and thereabouts that ditty speaks of. Lady Inger Gyldenlove is nigh on fifty, and wily to boot beyond all women. It will be no light matter to overcome her. But it must be done—at any cost. If I succeed in winning certain advantages over her that the King has long desired, I can reckon on the embassy to France next spring. You know that I spent three years at the University in Paris? My whole soul is bent on coming thither again, most of all if I can appear in lofty place, a king's ambassador. —Well, then—is it agreed? —do you leave Lady Inger to me? Remember—when you were last at Court in Copenhagen, I made way for you with more than one fair lady— —

JENS BIELKE. Nay, truly now—that generosity cost you little; one and all of them were at your beck and call. But let that pass; now that I have begun amiss in this matter, I had as lief that you should take it on your shoulders. One thing, though, you must promise—if the young Count Sture be in Ostrat, you will deliver him into my hands, dead or alive!

NILS LYKKE. You shall have him all alive. I, at any rate, mean not to kill him. But now you must ride back and join your people. Keep guard on the road. Should I mark aught that mislikes me, you shall know it forthwith.

JENS BIELKE. Good, good. But how am I to get out?

NILS LYKKE. The fellow that brought us in will show the way. But go quietly.

JENS BIELKE. Of course, of course. Well—good fortune to you!

NILS LYKKE. Fortune has never failed me in a war with women. Haste you now!

(JENS BIELKE goes out to the right.)

NILS LYKKE (stands still for a while; then walks about the room, looking round him; at last he says softly). So I am at Ostrat at last—the ancient seat that a child, two years ago, told me so much of. Lucia. Ay, two years ago she was still a child. And now—now she is dead. (Hums with a half-smile.) "Blossoms plucked are blossoms withered— — — —" (Looks round him again.) Ostrat. 'Tis as though I had seen it all before; as though I were at home here. —In there is the Banquet Hall. And underneath is—the grave-vault. It must be there that Lucia lies. (In a lower voice, half seriously, half with forced gaiety.) Were I timorous, I might well find myself fancying that when I set foot within Ostrat gate she turned about in her coffin; as I walked across the courtyard she lifted the lid; and when I named her name but now, 'twas as though a voice summoned her forth from the grave-vault. —Maybe she is even now groping her way up the stairs. The face-cloth blinds her, but she gropes on and on in spite of it. Now she has reached the Banquet Hall; she stands watching me from behind the door! (Turns his head backwards over one shoulder, nods, and says aloud:) Come nearer, Lucia! Talk to me a little! Your mother keeps me waiting. 'Tis tedious waiting—and you have helped me to while away many a tedious hour—— —— (Passes his hand over his forehead, and takes one or two turns up and down.) Ah, there! —Right, right; there is the the deep curtained window. It is there that Inger Gyldenlove is wont to stand gazing out over the road, as though looking for one that never comes. In there— (looks towards the door on the left)—somewhere in there is Sister Elina's chamber. Elina? Ay, Elina is her name. Can it be that she is so rare a being—so wise and so brave as Lucia drew her? Fair, too, they say. But for a wedded wife——? I should not have written so plainly—— —— (Lost in thought, he is on the point of sitting down by the table, but stands up again.) How will Lady Inger receive me? She will scarce burn the castle over our heads, or slip me through a trap-door. A stab from behind——? No, not that way either—— (Listens towards the hall.) Aha!

(LADY INGER GYLDENLOVE enters from the hall.)

LADY INGER (coldly). My greeting to you, Sir Councillor——

NILS LYKKE (bows deeply). Ah—the Lady of Ostrat!

LADY INGER. And thanks that you have forewarned me of your visit.

NILS LYKKE. I could do no less. I had reason to think that my coming might surprise you——

LADY INGER. In truth, Sir Councillor, you thought right there. Nils Lykke was certainly the last guest I looked to see at Ostrat.

NILS LYKKE. And still less, mayhap, did you think to see him come as a friend?

LADY INGER. As a friend? You add insult to all the shame and sorrow you have heaped upon my house? After bringing my child to the grave, you still dare— —

NILS LYKKE. With your leave, Lady Inger Gyldenlove—on that matter we should scarce agree; for you count as nothing what *I* lost by that same unhappy chance. I purposed nought but in honour. I was tired of my unbridled life; my thirtieth year was already past; I longed to mate me with a good and gentle wife. Add to all this the hope of becoming *your* son-in-law— —

LADY INGER. Beware, Sir Councillor! I have done all in my power to hide my child's unhappy fate. But because it is out of sight, think not it is out of mind. It may yet happen— —

NILS LYKKE. You threaten me, Lady Inger? I have offered you my hand in amity; you refuse to take it. Henceforth, then, it is to be open war between us?

LADY INGER. Was there ever aught else?

NILS LYKKE. Not on *your* side, mayhap. *I* have never been your enemy, —though as a subject of the King of Denmark I lacked not good cause.

LADY INGER. I understand you. I have not been pliant enough. It has not proved so easy as some of you hoped to lure me over into your camp. — Yet methinks you have nought to complain of. My daughter Merete's husband is your countryman—further I cannot go. My position is no easy one, Nils Lykke!

NILS LYKKE. That I can well believe. Both nobles and people here in Norway think they have an ancient claim on you—a claim, 'tis said, you have but half fulfilled.

LADY INGER. Your pardon, Sir Councillor, —I account for my doings to none but God and myself. If it please you, then, let me understand what brings you hither.

NILS LYKKE. Gladly, Lady Inger! The purport of my mission to this country can scarce be unknown to you— —?

LADY INGER. I know the mission that report assigns you. Our King would fain know how the Norwegian nobles stand affected towards him.

NILS LYKKE. Assuredly.

LADY INGER. Then that is why you visit Ostrat?

NILS LYKKE. In part. But it is far from my purpose to demand any profession of loyalty from you— —

LADY INGER. What then?

NILS LYKKE. Hearken to me, Lady Inger! You said yourself but now that your position is no easy one. You stand half way between two hostile camps, neither of which dares trust you fully. Your own interest must needs bind you to *us*. On the other hand, you are bound to the disaffected by the bond of nationality, and—who knows? —mayhap by some secret tie as well.

LADY INGER (aside). A secret tie! Christ, does he— —?

NILS LYKKE (notices her emotion, but makes no sign and continues without change of manner). You cannot but see that such a position must ere long become impossible. —Suppose, now, it lay in my power to free you from these embarrassments which— —

LADY INGER. In your power, you say?

NILS LYKKE. First of all, Lady Inger, I would beg you to lay no stress on any careless words I may have used concerning that which lies between us two. Think not that I have forgotten for a moment the wrong I have done you. Suppose, now, I had long purposed to make atonement, as far as might be, where I had sinned. Suppose that were my reason for undertaking this mission.

LADY INGER. Speak your meaning more clearly, Sir Councillor; —I cannot follow you.

NILS LYKKE. I can scarce be mistaken in thinking that you, as well as I, know of the threatened troubles in Sweden. You know, or at least you can guess, that this rising is of far wider aim than is commonly supposed, and you understand therefore that our King cannot look on quietly and let things take their course. Am I not right?

LADY INGER. Go on.

NILS LYKKE (searchingly, after a short pause). There is one possible chance that might endanger Gustav Vasa's throne— —

LADY INGER (aside). Whither is he tending?

NILS LYKKE. — —the chance, namely, that there should exist in Sweden a man entitled by his birth to claim election to the kingship.

LADY INGER (evasively). The Swedish nobles have been even as bloodily hewn down as our own, Sir Councillor. Where would you seek for— —?

NILS LYKKE (with a smile). Seek? The man is found already— —

LADY INGER (starts violently). Ah! He is found?

NILS LYKKE. — —And he is too closely akin to you, Lady Inger, to be far from your thoughts at this moment. (Looks at her.) The last Count Sture left a son— —

LADY INGER (with a cry). Holy Saviour, how know you— —?

NILS LYKKE (surprised). Be calm, Madam, and let me finish. — This young man has lived quietly till now with his mother, Sten Sture's widow.

LADY INGER (breathes more freely). With— —? Ah, yes—true, true!

NILS LYKKE. But now he has come forward openly. He has shown himself in the Dales as leader of the peasants; their numbers are growing day by day; and—as perhaps you know—they are finding friends among the peasants on this side of the border-hills.

LADY INGER (who has in the meantime regained her composure). Sir Councillor, —you speak of all these things as though they must of necessity be known to me. What ground have I given you to believe so? I know, and wish to know, nothing. All my care is to live quietly within my own domain; I give no helping hand to the rebels; but neither must you count on me if it be your purpose to put them down.

NILS LYKKE (in a low voice). Would you still be inactive, if it were my purpose to stand by them?

LADY INGER. How am I to understand you?

NILS LYKKE. Have you not seen whither I have been aiming all this time? —Well, I will tell you all, honestly and straightforwardly. Know, then, that the King and his Council see clearly that we can have no sure footing in Norway so long as the nobles and the people continue, as now, to think themselves wronged and oppressed. We understand to the full that willing allies are better than sullen subjects; and we have therefore no heartier wish than to loosen the bonds that hamper *us*, in effect, quite as straitly as you. But you will scarce deny that the temper of Norway towards us makes such a step too dangerous—so long as we have no sure support behind us.

LADY INGER. And this support——?

NILS LYKKE. Should naturally come from Sweden. But, mark well, not so long as Gustav Vasa holds the helm; *his* reckoning with Denmark is not settled yet, and mayhap never will be. But a new king of Sweden, who had the people with him, and who owed his throne to the help of Denmark—— —— Well, you begin to understand me? *Then* we could safely say to you Norwegians: "Take back your old ancestral rights; choose you a ruler after your own mind; be our friends in need, as we will be in yours! "—Mark you well, Lady Inger, herein is our generosity less than it may seem; for you must see that, far from weakening, 'twill rather strengthen us. And now I have opened my heart to you so fully, do you too cast away all mistrust. And therefore (confidently)—the knight from Sweden, who came hither an hour before me——

LADY INGER. Then you already know of his coming?

NILS LYKKE. Most certainly. It is him I seek.

LADY INGER (to herself). Strange! It must be as Olaf Skaktavl said. (To NILS LYKKE.) I pray you wait here, Sir Councillor! I go to bring him to you.

(Goes out through the Banquet Hall.)

NILS LYKKE (looks after her a while in exultant astonishment). She is bringing him! Ay, truly—she is bringing him! The battle is half won. I little thought it would go so smoothly— — She is deep in the counsels of the rebels; she started in terror when I named Sten Sture's son— — And now? Hm! Since Lady Inger has been simple enough to walk into the snare, Nils Sture will not make many difficulties. A hot-blooded boy, thoughtless and rash— — — — With my promise of help he will set forth at once—unhappily Jens Bielke will snap him up by the way—and the whole rising will be nipped in the bud. And then? Then one step more in our own behalf. It is spread abroad that the young Count Sture has been at Ostrat, —that a Danish envoy has had audience of Lady Inger—that thereupon the young Count Nils has been snapped up by King Gustav's men-at-arms a mile from the castle— — — — Let Inger Gyldenlove's name among the people stand never so high—it will scarce recover from such a blow. (Starts up in sudden uneasiness.) By all the devils— —! What if she has scented mischief! It may be he is slipping through our fingers even now— — (Listens toward the hall, and says with relief.) Ah, there is no fear. Here they come.

(LADY INGER GYLDENLOVE enters from the hall along with OLAF SKAKTAVL.)

LADY INGER (to NILS LYKKE). Here is the man you seek.

NILS LYKKE (aside). In the name of hell—what means this?

LADY INGER. I have told this knight your name and all that you have imparted to me— —

NILS LYKKE (irresolutely). Ay? Have you so? Well— —

LADY INGER— — And I will not hide from you that his faith in your help is none of the strongest.

NILS LYKKE. Is it not?

LADY INGER. Can you marvel at that? You know, surely, both the cause he fights for and his bitter fate— —

NILS LYKKE. This man's— —? Ah—yes, truly— —

OLAF SKAKTAVL (to NILS LYKKE). But seeing 'tis Peter Kanzler himself that has appointed us this meeting— —

NILS LYKKE. Peter Kanzler— —? (Recovers himself quickly.) Ay, right, —I have a mission from Peter Kanzler— —

OLAF SKAKTAVL. He must know best whom he can trust. So why should I trouble my head with thinking how— —

NILS LYKKE. Ay, you are right, noble Sir; that were folly indeed.

OLAF SKAKTAVL. Rather let us come straight to the matter.

NILS LYKKE. Straight to the point; no beating about the bush— 'tis ever my fashion.

OLAF SKAKTAVL. Then will you tell me your mission here?

NILS LYKKE. Methinks you can partly guess my errand— —

OLAF SKAKTAVL. Peter Kanzler said something of papers that— —

NILS LYKKE. Papers? Ay, true, the papers!

OLAF SKAKTAVL. Doubtless you have them with you?

NILS LYKKE. Of course; safely bestowed; so safely that I cannot at once— — (Appears to search the inner pockets of his doublet; says to himself:) Who the devil is he? What pretext shall I make? I may be on the brink of great discoveries— — (Notices that the Servants are laying the table and lighting the lamps in the Banquet Hall, and says to OLAF SKAKTAVL:) Ah, I see Lady Inger has taken order for the evening meal. We could perhaps better talk of our affairs at table.

OLAF SKAKTAVL. Good; as you will.

NILS LYKKE (aside). Time gained—all gained! (To LADY INGER with a show of great friendliness.) And meanwhile we might learn what part Lady Inger Gyldenlove purposes to take in our design?

LADY INGER. I? —None.

NILS LYKKE AND OLAF SKAKTAVL. None!

LADY INGER. Can ye marvel, noble Sirs, that I venture not on a game, wherein all is staked on one cast? And that, too, when none of my allies dare trust me fully.

NILS LYKKE. That reproach touches not me. I trust you blindly; I pray you be assured of that.

OLAF SKAKTAVL. Who should believe in you, if not your countrymen?

LADY INGER. Truly, —this confidence rejoices me.

(Goes to a cupboard in the back wall and fills two goblets with wine.)

NILS LYKKE (aside). Curse her, will she slip out of the noose?

LADY INGER (hands a goblet to each). And since so it is, I offer you a cup of welcome to Ostrat. Drink, noble knights! Pledge me to the last drop! (Looks from one to the other after they have drunk, and says gravely:) But now I must tell you—one goblet held a welcome for my friend; the other—death for my enemy.

NILS LYKKE (throws down the goblet). Ah, I am poisoned!

OLAF SKAKTAVL (at the same time, clutches his sword). Death and hell, have you murdered me?

LADY INGER (to OLAF SKAKTAVL, pointing to NILS LYKKE.) You see the Danes' trust in Inger Gyldenlove— — (To NILS LYKKE, pointing to OLAF SKAKTAVL.) — —and likewise my countrymen's faith in me! (To both of them.) And I am to place myself in your power? Gently, noble Sirs— gently! The Lady of Ostrat is not yet in her dotage.

(ELINA GYLDENLOVE enters by the door on the left.)

ELINA. I heard voices! What is amiss?

LADY INGER (to NILS LYKKE). My daughter Elina.

NILS LYKKE (softly). Elina! I had not pictured her thus.

(ELINA catches sight of NILS LYKKE, and stands still, as in surprise, gazing at him.)

LADY INGER (touches her arm). My child—this knight is— —

ELINA (motions her mother back with her hand, still looking intently at him, and says:) There is no need! I see who he is. He is Nils Lykke.

NILS LYKKE (aside, to LADY INGER). How? Does she know me? Can Lucia have— —? Can she know— —?

LADY INGER. Hush! She knows nothing.

ELINA (to herself). I knew it; —even so must Nils Lykke appear.

NILS LYKKE (approaches her). Yes, Elina Gyldenlove, —you have guessed rightly. And as it seems that, in some sense, you know me, —and moreover, as I am your mother's guest, —you will not deny me the flower-spray you wear in your bosom. So long as it is fresh and fragrant I shall have in it an image of yourself.

ELINA (proudly, but still gazing at him). Pardon me, Sir Knight— it was plucked in my own chamber, and *there* can grow no flower for you.

NILS LYKKE (loosening a spray of flowers that he wears in the front of his doublet). At least you will not disdain this humble gift. 'Twas a farewell token from a courtly lady when I set forth from Trondhiem this morning. —But mark me, noble maiden, —were I to offer you a gift that were fully worthy of you, it could be naught less than a princely crown.

ELINA (who has taken the flowers passively). And were it the royal crown of Denmark you held forth to me—before I shared it with *you*, I would crush it to pieces between my hands, and cast the fragments at your feet!

(Throws down the flowers at his feet, and goes into the Banquet Hall.)

OLAF SKAKTAVL (mutters to himself). Bold—as Inger Ottisdaughter by Knut Alfson's bier!

LADY INGER (softly, after looking alternately at ELINA and NILS LYKKE). The wolf *can* be tamed. Now to forge the fetters.

NILS LYKKE (picks up the flowers and gazes in rapture after ELINA). God's holy blood, but she is proud and fair

ACT THIRD.

(The Banquet Hall. A high bow-window in the background; a smaller window in front on the left. Several doors on each side. The roof is supported by massive wooden pillars, on which, as well as on the walls, are hung all sorts of weapons. Pictures of saints, knights, and ladies hang in long rows. Pendent from the roof a large many-branched lamp, alight. In front, on the right, an ancient carven high-seat. In the middle of the hall, a table with the remnants of the evening meal.)

(ELINA GYLDENLOVE enters from the left, slowly and in deep thought. Her expression shows that she is going over again in her mind the scene with NILS LYKKE. At last she repeats the motion with which she flung away the flowers, and says in a low voice:)

ELINA. —— ——And then he gathered up the fragments of the crown of Denmark—no, 'twas the flowers—and: "God's holy blood, but she is proud and fair! " Had he whispered the words in the remotest corner, long leagues from Ostrat, —still had I heard them! How I hate him! How I have always hated him, —this Nils Lykke! — There lives not another man like him, 'tis said. He plays with women—and treads them under his feet. And it was to him my mother thought to offer me! —How I hate him! They say Nils Lykke is unlike all other men. It is not true! There is nothing strange in him. There are many, many like him! When Biorn used to tell me his tales, all the princes looked as Nils Lykke looks. When I sat lonely here in the hall and dreamed my histories, and my knights came and went, —they were one and all even as he. How strange and how good it is to hate! Never have I known how sweet it can be—till to-night. Ah—not to live a thousand years would I sell the moments I have lived since I saw him! — "God's holy blood, but she is proud—— ——"

(Goes slowly towards the background, opens the window and looks out. NILS LYKKE comes in by the first door on the right.)

NILS LYKKE (to himself). "Sleep well at Ostrat, Sir Knight, " said Inger Gyldenlove as she left me. Sleep well? Ay, it is easily said, but—— —— Out there, sky and sea in tumult; below, in the grave-vault, a young girl on her bier; the fate of two kingdoms in my hand; and in my breast a withered flower that a woman has flung at my feet. Truly, I fear me sleep will be slow of coming. (Notices ELINA, who has left the window, and is going out on the left.) There she is. Her haughty eyes seem veiled with thought. —Ah, if I but dared—(aloud). Mistress Elina!

ELINA (stops at the door). What will you? Why do you pursue me?

NILS LYKKE. You err; I pursue you not. I am myself pursued.

ELINA. You?

NILS LYKKE. By a multitude of thoughts. Therefore 'tis with sleep as with you: —it flees me.

ELINA. Go to the window, and there you will find pastime; —a storm-tossed sea— —

NILS LYKKE (smiles). A storm-tossed sea? That I may find in you as well.

ELINA. In me?

NILS LYKKE. Ay, of that our first meeting has assured me.

ELINA. And that offends you?

NILS LYKKE. Nay, in nowise; yet I could wish to see you of milder mood.

ELINA (proudly). Think you that you will ever have your wish?

NILS LYKKE. I am sure of it. I have a welcome word to say to you.

ELINA. What is it?

NILS LYKKE. Farewell.

ELINA (comes a step nearer him). Farewell? You are leaving Ostrat—so soon?

NILS LYKKE. This very night.

ELINA (seems to hesitate for a moment; then says coldly:) Then take my greeting, Sir Knight! (Bows and is about to go.)

NILS LYKKE. Elina Gyldenlove, —I have no right to keep you here; but 'twill be unlike your nobleness if you refuse to hear what I have to say to you.

ELINA. I hear you, Sir Knight.

NILS LYKKE. I know you hate me.

ELINA. You are keen-sighted, I perceive.

NILS LYKKE. But I know, too, that I have fully merited your hate. Unseemly and insolent were the words I wrote of you in my letter to Lady Inger.

ELINA. It may be; I have not read them.

NILS LYKKE. But at least their purport is not unknown to you; I know your mother has not left you in ignorance of the matter; at the least she has told you how I praised the lot of the man who— —; surely you know the hope I nursed— —

ELINA. Sir Knight—if it is of that you would speak— —

NILS LYKKE. I speak of it only to excuse what I have done; for no other reason, I swear to you. If my fame has reached you—as I have too much cause of fear—before I myself set foot in Ostrat, you must needs know enough of my life not to wonder that in such things I should go to work something boldly. I have met many women, Elina Gyldenlove; but not one have I found unyielding. Such lessons, look you, teach a man to be secure. He loses the habit of roundabout ways— —

ELINA. May be so. I know not of what metal those women can have been. For the rest, you err in thinking 'twas your letter to my mother that aroused my soul's hatred and bitterness against you. It is of older date.

NILS LYKKE (uneasily). Of older date? What mean you?

ELINA. 'Tis as you guessed: —your fame has gone before you to Ostrat, even as over all the land. Nils Lykke's name is never spoken save with the name of some woman whom he has beguiled and cast off. Some speak it in wrath, others with laughter and wanton jeering at those weak-souled creatures. But through the wrath and the laughter and the jeers rings the song they have made of you, masterful and insolent as an enemy's song of triumph. 'Tis all this that has begotten my hate for you. Your were ever in my thoughts, and I longed to meet you face to face, that you might learn that there are women on whom your soft speeches are lost—if you should think to use them.

NILS LYKKE. You judge me unjustly, if you judge from what rumour has told of me. Even if there be truth in all you have heard, — you know not the causes that have made me what I am. —As a boy of seventeen I began my course of pleasure. I have lived full fifteen years since then. Light women granted me all that I would—even before the wish had shaped itself into a prayer; and what I offered them they seized with eager hands. You are the first woman that has flung back a gift of mine with scorn at my feet. Think not I reproach you. Rather I honour you for it, as never before have I honoured woman. But for this I reproach my fate— and the thought is a gnawing pain to me—that I did not meet you sooner— — — — Elina Gyldenlove! Your mother has told me of you. While far from Ostrat life ran its restless course, you went your lonely way in silence, living in your dreams and histories. Therefore you will understand what I have to tell you. —Know, then, that once I too lived even such a life as yours. Methought that when I stepped forth into the great world, a noble and stately woman would come to meet me, and would beckon me to her and point me the path towards a lofty goal. —I was deceived, Elina Gyldenlove! Women came to meet me; but *she* was not among them. Ere yet I had come to full manhood, I had learnt to despise them all. Was it my fault? Why were not the others even as you? —I know the fate of your fatherland lies heavy on your soul, and you know the part I have in these affairs— — — — 'Tis said of me that I am false as the sea-foam. Mayhap I am; but if I be, it is women who have made me so. Had I sooner found what I sought, —had I met a woman proud and noble and high-souled even as you, then had my path been different indeed. At this moment, maybe, I had been standing at your side as the champion of all that suffer wrong in Norway's land. For *this* I believe: a woman is the mightiest power in the world, and in her hand it lies to guide a man whither God Almighty would have him go.

ELINA (to herself). Can it be as he says? Nay nay; there is falsehood in his eyes and deceit on his lips. And yet—no song is sweeter than his words.

NILS LYKKE (coming closer, speaks low and more intimately). How often, when you have been sitting here at Ostrat, alone with your changeful thoughts, have you felt your bosom stifling; how often have the roof and walls seemed to shrink together till they crushed your very soul. Then have your longings taken wing with you; then have you yearned to fly far from here, you knew not whither. —How often have you not wandered alone by the fiord; far out a ship has sailed by in fair array, with knights and ladies on her deck with song and music of stringed instruments; —a faint, far-off rumour of great events has reached your ears; —and you have felt a longing in your breast, an unconquerable craving to know all that lies beyond the sea. But you have not understood what ailed you. At times you have thought it was the fate of your fatherland that filled you with all these restless broodings. You deceived yourself; —a maiden so young as you has other food for musing— — — — Elina Gyldenlove! Have you never had visions of an unknown power—a strong mysterious might, that binds together the destinies of mortals? When you dreamed of knightly jousts and joyous festivals—saw you never in your dreams a knight, who stood in the midst of the gayest rout, with a smile on his lips and with bitterness in his heart, —a knight that had once dreamed a dream as fair as yours, of a woman noble and stately, for whom he went ever seeking, and in vain?

ELINA. Who are you, that have power to clothe my most secret thought in words? How can you tell me what I have borne in my inmost soul—and knew it not myself? How know you— —?

NILS LYKKE. All that I have told you, I have read in your eyes.

ELINA. Never has any man spoken to me as you have. I have understood you but dimly; and yet—all, all seems changed since— — (To herself.) Now I understand why they said that Nils Lykke was unlike all other.

NILS LYKKE. There is one thing in the world that might drive a man to madness, but to think of it; and that is the thought of what might have been if things had fallen out in this way or that. Had I met you on my path while the tree of my life was yet green and budding, at this hour, mayhap, you had been— — — — But forgive me, noble lady! Our speech of these past few moments has made me forget how we stand one to another. 'Twas as though a secret voice had told me from the first that to you I could speak openly, without flattery or dissimulation.

ELINA. That can you.

NILS LYKKE. 'Tis well; —and it may be that this openness has already in part reconciled us. Ay—my hope is yet bolder. The time may yet come when you will think of the stranger knight without hate or bitterness in your soul. Nay, —mistake me not! I mean not now— but some time, in the days to come. And that this may be the less hard for you—and as I have begun once for all to speak to you plainly and openly—let me tell you— —

ELINA. Sir Knight— —!

NILS LYKKE (smiling). Ah, I see the thought of my letter still affrights you. Fear nought on that score. I would from my heart it were unwritten, for—I know 'twill concern you little enough, so I may even say it right out—for I love you not, and shall never come to you. Fear nothing, therefore, as I said before; I shall in no wise seek to— — — — But what ails you— —?

ELINA. Me? Nothing, nothing. —Tell me but one thing. Why do you still wear those flowers? What would you with them?

NILS LYKKE. These? Are they not a gage of battle you have thrown down to the wicked Nils Lykke on behalf of all womankind? What could I do but take it up? You asked what I would with them. (Softly.) When I stand again amidst the fair ladies of Denmark—when the music of the strings is hushed and there is silence in the hall—then will I bring forth these flowers and tell a tale of a young maiden sitting alone in a gloomy black-beamed hall, far to the north in Norway— — (Breaks off and bows respectfully.) But I fear I keep the noble daughter of the house too long. We shall meet no more; for before day-break I shall be gone. So now I bid you farewell.

ELINA. Fare you well, Sir Knight!

(A short silence.)

NILS LYKKE. Again you are deep in thought, Elina Gyldenlove! Is it the fate of your fatherland that weighs upon you still?

ELINA (shakes her head, absently gazing straight in front of her). My fatherland? —I think not of my fatherland.

NILS LYKKE. Then 'tis the strife and misery of the time that cause you dread.

ELINA. The time? I have forgotten time—— —— You go to Denmark? Said you not so?

NILS LYKKE. I go to Denmark.

ELINA. Can I see towards Denmark from this hall?

NILS LYKKE (points to the window on the left). Ay, from this window. Denmark lies there, to the south.

ELINA. And is it far from here? More than a hundred miles?

NILS LYKKE. Much more. The sea lies between you and Denmark.

ELINA (to herself). The sea? Thought has seagull's wings. The sea cannot stay it.

(Goes out to the left.)

NILS LYKKE (looks after her awhile; then says:) If I could but spare two days now—or even one—I would have her in my power, even as the others. And yet is there rare stuff in this maiden. She is proud. Might I not after all——? No; rather humble her—— —— (Paces the room.) Verily, I believe she has set my blood on fire. Who would have thought it possible after all these years? —Enough of this! I must get out of the tangle I am entwined in here. (Sits in a chair on the right.) What is the meaning of it? Both Olaf Skaktavl and Inger Gyldenlove seem blind to the mistrust 'twill waken, when 'tis rumoured that I am in their league. —Or can Lady Inger have seen through my purpose? Can she have seen that all my promises were but designed to lure Nils Sture forth from his hiding-place? (Springs up.) Damnation! Is it I that have been fooled? 'Tis like enough that Count Sture is not at Ostrat at all? It may be the rumour of his flight was but a feint. He may be safe and sound among his friends in

Sweden, while I— — (Walks restlessly up and down.) And to think I was so sure of success! If I should effect nothing? If Lady Inger should penetrate my designs—and publish my discomfiture— — To be a laughing-stock both here and in Denmark! To have sought to lure Lady Inger into a trap—and given her cause the help it most needed—strengthened her in the people's favour— —! Ah, I could well-nigh sell myself to the Evil One, would he but help me to lay hands on Count Sture.

(The window in the background is pushed open. NILS STENSSON is seen outside.)

NILS LYKKE (clutches at his sword). What now?

NILS STENSSON (jumps down on to the floor). Ah; here I am at last then!

NILS LYKKE (aside). What means this?

NILS STENSSON. God's peace, master!

NILS LYKKE. Thanks, good Sir! Methinks yo have chosen a strange mode of entrance.

NILS STENSSON. Ay, what the devil was I to do? The gate was shut. Folk must sleep in this house like bears at Yuletide.

NILS LYKKE. God be thanked! Know you not that a good conscience is the best pillow?

NILS STENSSON. Ay, it must be even so; for all my rattling and thundering, I— —

NILS LYKKE. — —You won not in?

NILS STENSSON. You have hit it. So I said to myself: As you are bidden to be in Ostrat to-night, if you have to go through fire and water, you may surely make free to creep through a window.

NILS LYKKE (aside). Ah, if it should be— —! (Moves a step or two nearer.) Was it, then, of the last necessity that you should reach Ostrat to-night?

NILS STENSSON. Was it? Ay, faith but it was. I love not to keep folk waiting, I can tell you.

NILS LYKKE. Aha, —then Lady Inger Gyldenlove looks for your coming?

NILS STENSSON. Lady Inger Gyldenlove? Nay, that I can scarce say for certain; (with a sly smile) but there might be some one else— —

NILS LYKKE (smiles in answer). Ah, so there might be some one else?

NILS STENSSON. Tell me—are you of the house?

NILS LYKKE. I? Well, in so far that I am Lady Inger's guest this evening.

NILS STENSSON. A guest? —Is not to-night the third night after Martinmas?

NILS LYKKE. The third night after— —? Ay, right enough. —Would you seek the lady of the house at once? I think she is not yet gone to rest. But might you not sit down and rest awhile, dear young Sir? See, here is yet a flagon of wine remaining, and doubtless you will find some food. Come, fall to; you will do wisely to refresh your strength.

NILS STENSSON. You are right, Sir; 'twere not amiss. (Sits down by the table and eats and drinks.) Both roast meat and sweet cakes! Why, you live like lords here! When one has slept, as I have, on the naked ground, and lived on bread and water for four or five days— —

NILS LYKKE (looks at him with a smile). Ay, such a life must be hard for one that is wont to sit at the high-table in noble halls— —

NILS STENSSON. Noble halls— —?

NILS LYKKE. But now can you take your rest at Ostrat, as long as it likes you.

NILS STENSSON (pleased). Ay? Can I truly? Then I am not to begone again so soon?

NILS LYKKE. Nay, that I know not. Sure you yourself can best say that.

NILS STENSSON (softly). Oh, the devil! (Stretches himself in the chair.) Well, you see—'tis not yet certain. I, for my part, were nothing loath to stay quiet here awhile; but——

NILS LYKKE. ——But you are not in all points your own master? There be other duties and other circumstances——?

NILS STENSSON. Ay, that is just the rub. Were I to choose, I would rest me at Ostrat at least the winter through; I have seldom led aught but a soldier's life—— (Interrupts himself suddenly, fills a goblet, and drinks.) Your health, Sir!

NILS LYKKE. A soldier's life? Hm!

NILS STENSSON. Nay, what I would have said is this: I have been eager to see Lady Inger Gyldenlove, whose fame has spread so wide. She must be a queenly woman, —is't not so? —The one thing I like not in her, is that she shrinks so cursedly from open action.

NILS LYKKE. From open action?

NILS STENSSON. Ay ay, you understand me; I mean she is so loath to take a hand in driving the foreign rulers out of the land.

NILS LYKKE. Ay, you are right. But if you do your best now, you will doubtless work her to your will.

NILS STENSSON. I? God knows it would but little serve if *I*——

NILS LYKKE. Yet 'tis strange you should seek her here if you have so little hope.

NILS STENSSON. What mean you? —Tell me, know you Lady Inger?

NILS LYKKE. Surely; I am her guest, and——

NILS STENSSON. Ay, but it does not at all follow that you know her. I too am her guest, yet have I never seen so much as her shadow.

NILS LYKKE. Yet did you speak of her— —

NILS STENSSON. — —As all folk speak. Why should I not? And besides, I have often enough heard from Peter Kanzler— —

(Stops in confusion, and begins eating again.)

NILS LYKKE. You would have said— —?

NILS STENSSON (eating). I? Nay, 'tis all one.

(NILS LYKKE laughs.)

NILS STENSSON. Why laugh you, Sir?

NILS LYKKE. 'Tis nought, Sir!

NILS STENSSON (drinks). A pretty vintage ye have in this house.

NILS LYKKE (approaches him confidentially). Listen—were it not time now to throw off the mask?

NILS STENSSON (smiling). The mask? Why, do as seems best to you.

NILS LYKKE. Then off with all disguise. You are known, Count Sture!

NILS STENSSON (with a laugh). Count Sture? Do you too take me for Count Sture? (Rises from the table.) You mistake, Sir; I am not Count Sture.

NILS LYKKE. You are not? Then who are you?

NILS STENSSON. My name is Nils Stensson.

NILS LYKKE (looks at him with a smile). Hm! Nils Stensson? But you are not Sten Sture's son Nils? The name chimes at least.

NILS STENSSON. True enough; but God knows what right I have to bear it. My father I never knew; my mother was a poor peasant-woman, that was robbed and murdered in one of the old feuds. Peter Kanzler chanced to be on the spot; he took me into his care, brought me up, and taught me the trade of arms. As you know, King Gustav has been hunting him this many a year; and I have followed him faithfully, wherever he went.

NILS LYKKE. Peter Kanzler has taught you more than the trade of arms, meseems— — — — Well, well; then you are not Nils Sture. But at least you come from Sweden. Peter Kanzler has sent you here to find a stranger, who— —

NILS STENSSON (nods cunningly). — —Who is found already.

NILS LYKKE (somewhat uncertain). And whom you do not know?

NILS STENSSON. As little as you know me; for I swear to you by God himself: I am not Count Sture!

NILS LYKKE. In sober earnest, Sir?

NILS STENSSON. As truly as I live! Wherefore should I deny it, if I were?

NILS LYKKE. Then where is Count Sture?

NILS STENSSON (in a low voice). Ay, *that* is just the secret.

NILS LYKKE (whispers). Which is known to you, is it not?

NILS STENSSON (nods). And which I have to tell to you.

NILS LYKKE. To me? Well then, —where is he?

(NILS STENSSON points upwards.)

NILS LYKKE. Up there? Lady Inger holds him hidden in the loft-room?

NILS STENSSON. Nay, nay; you mistake me. (Looks round cautiously.) Nils Sture is in Heaven!

NILS LYKKE. Dead? And where?

NILS STENSSON. In his mother's castle, —three weeks since.

NILS LYKKE. Ah, you are deceiving me! 'Tis but five or six days since he crossed the frontier into Norway.

NILS STENSSON. Oh, that was I.

NILS LYKKE. But just before that the Count had appeared in the Dales. The people were restless already, and on his coming they broke out openly and would have chosen him for king.

NILS STENSSON. Ha-ha-ha; that was me too!

NILS LYKKE. You?

NILS STENSSON. I will tell you how it came about. One day Peter Kanzler called me to him and gave me to know that great things were preparing. He bade me set out for Norway and go to Ostrat, where I must be on a certain fixed day— —

NILS LYKKE (nods). The third night after Martinmas.

NILS STENSSON. I was to meet a stranger there— —

NILS LYKKE. Ay, right; I am he.

NILS STENSSON. He was to tell me what more I had to do. Moreover, I was to let him know that the Count was dead of a sudden, but that as yet 'twas known to no one save to his mother the Countess, together with Peter Kanzler and a few old servants of the Stures.

NILS LYKKE. I understand. The Count was the peasants' rallying-point. Were the tidings of his death to spread, they would fall asunder, —and the whole project would come to nought.

NILS STENSSON. Ay, maybe so; I know little of such matters.

NILS LYKKE. But how came you to give yourself out for the Count?

NILS STENSSON. How came I to— —? Nay, what know I? Many's the mad prank I've hit on in my day. And yet 'twas not I hit on it neither; wherever I appeared in the Dales, the people crowded round me and greeted me as Count Sture. Deny it as I pleased, —'twas wasted breath. The Count had been there two years before, they said—and the veriest child knew me again. Well, be it so, thought I; never again will you be a Count in this life; why not try what 'tis like for once?

NILS LYKKE. Well, —and what did you more?

NILS STENSSON. I? I ate and drank and took my ease. Pity 'twas that I must away again so soon. But when I set forth across the frontier—ha-ha-ha—I promised them I would soon be back with three or four thousand men—I know not how many I said—and then we would lay on in earnest.

NILS LYKKE. And you did not bethink you that you were acting rashly?

NILS STENSSON. Ay, afterwards; but then, to be sure, 'twas too late.

NILS LYKKE. It grieves me for you, my young friend; but you will soon come to feel the effects of your folly. Let me tell you that you are pursued. A troop of Swedish men-at-arms is out after you.

NILS STENSSON. After me? Ha-ha-ha. Nay, that is rare! And when they come and think they have Count Sture in their clutches— ha-ha-ha!

NILS LYKKE (gravely). ——Then farewell to your life.

NILS STENSSON. My——? But I am not Count Sture.

NILS LYKKE. You have called the people to arms. You have given seditious promises, and raised troubles in the land.

NILS STENSSON. Ay, but 'twas only in jest!

NILS LYKKE. King Gustav will scarce look on the matter in that light.

NILS STENSSON. Truly, there is something in what you say. To think I could be such a madman—— —— Well well, I'm not a dead man yet! You will protect me; and besides—the men-at-arms can scarce be at my heels.

NILS LYKKE. But what else have you to tell me?

NILS STENSSON. I? Nothing. When once I have given you the packet— —

NILS LYKKE (unguardedly). The packet?

NILS STENSSON. Ay, sure you know— —

NILS LYKKE. Ah, right, right; the papers from Peter Kanzler— —

NILS STENSSON. See, here they all are.

(Takes out a packet from inside his doublet, and hands it to NILS LYKKE.)

NILS LYKKE (aside). Letters and papers for Olaf Skaktavl. (To NILS STENSSON.) The packet is open, I see. 'Tis like you know what it contains?

NILS STENSSON. No, good sir; I am ill at reading writing; and for reason good.

NILS LYKKE. I understand; you have given most care to the trade of arms. (Sits down by the table on the right, and runs through the papers.) Aha! Here is light enough and to spare on what is brewing. This small letter tied with a silken thread— — (Examines the address.) This too for Olaf Skaktavl. (Opens the letter, and glances through its contents.) From Peter Kanzler. I thought as much. (Reads under his breath.) "I am hard bested, for— —; ay, sure enough; here it stands, —"Young Count Sture has been gathered to his fathers, even at the time fixed for the revolt to break forth" —" —but all may yet be made good— —" What now? (Reads on in astonishment.) "You must know, then, Olaf Skaktavl, that the young man who brings you this letter is a son of— —" Heaven and earth—can it be so? —Ay, by Christ's blood, even so 'tis written! (Glances at NILS STENSSON.) Can he be— —? Ah, if it were so! (Reads on.) "I have nurtured him since he was a year old; but up to this day I have ever refused to give him back, trusting to have in him a sure hostage for Inger Gyldenlove's faithfulness to us and to our friends. Yet in that respect he has been of but little service to us. You may marvel that I told you not this secret when you were with me here of late; therefore will I confess freely that I feared you might seize upon him, even as I had done. But now, when you have seen Lady Inger, and have doubtless assured yourself how loath she is to have a hand in our undertaking, you will see that 'tis wisest to give her back her own as soon as may be. Well might it come to pass that in her joy and security and thankfulness—" —— "—that is now our last hope. " (Sits for awhile as though struck dumb with surprise; then exclaims in a low voice:) Aha, —what a letter! Gold would not buy it!

NILS STENSSON. 'Tis plain I have brought you weighty tidings. Ay, ay, —Peter Kanzler has many irons in the fire, folk say.

NILS LYKKE (to himself). What to do with all this? A thousand paths are open to me—— Suppose I——? No, 'twere to risk too much. But if—ah, if I——? I will venture it. (Tears the letter across, crumples up the pieces, and hides them inside his doublet; puts back the other papers into the packet, which he sticks inside his belt; rises and says:) A word, my friend!

NILS STENSSON. Well—your looks say that the game goes bravely.

NILS LYKKE. Ay, by my soul it does. You have given me a hand of nought but court cards, —queens and knaves and——

NILS STENSSON. But what of me, that have brought all these good tidings? Have I nought more to do?

NILS LYKKE. You? Ay, that have you. You belong to the game. You are a king—and king of trumps too.

NILS STENSSON. I a king? Oh, now I understand; you are thinking of my exaltation——

NILS LYKKE. Your exaltation?

NILS STENSSON. Ay; that which you foretold me, if King Gustav's men got me in their clutches——

(Makes a motion to indicate hanging.)

NILS LYKKE. True enough; —but let that trouble you no more. It now lies with yourself alone whether within a month you shall have the hempen noose or a chain of gold about your neck.

NILS STENSSON. A chain of gold? And it lies with me?

(NILS LYKKE nods.)

NILS STENSSON. Why then, the devil take musing! Do you tell me what I am to do.

NILS LYKKE. I will. But first you must swear me a solemn oath that no living creature in the wide world shall know what I am to tell you.

NILS STENSSON. Is that all? You shall have ten oaths if you will.

NILS LYKKE. Not so lightly, young Sir! It is no jesting matter.

NILS STENSSON. Well well; I am grave enough.

NILS LYKKE. In the Dales you called yourself a Count's son; — is't not so?

NILS STENSSON. Nay—begin you now on that again? Have I not made free confession——

NILS LYKKE. You mistake me. What you said in the Dales was the truth.

NILS STENSSON. The truth? What mean you by that? Tell me but——!

NILS LYKKE. First your oath! The holiest, the most inviolable you can swear.

NILS STENSSON. That you shall have. Yonder on the wall hangs the picture of the Holy Virgin——

NILS LYKKE. The Holy Virgin has grown impotent of late. Know you not what the monk of Wittenberg maintains?

NILS STENSSON. Fie! how can you heed the monk of Wittenberg? Peter Kanzler says he is a heretic.

NILS LYKKE. Nay, let us not wrangle concerning him. Here can I show you a saint will serve full well to make oath to. (Points to a picture hanging on one of the panels.) Come hither, —swear that you will be silent till I myself release your tongue—silent, as you hope for Heaven's salvation for yourself and for the man whose picture hangs there.

NILS STENSSON (approaching the picture). I swear it—so help me God's holy word! (Falls back a step in amazement.) But—Christ save me——!

NILS LYKKE. What now?

NILS STENSSON. The picture——! Sure 'tis myself!

NILS LYKKE. 'Tis old Sten Sture, even as he lived and moved in his youthful years.

NILS STENSSON. Sten Sture! —And the likeness——? And—said you not I spoke the truth, when I called myself a Count's son? Was't not so?

NILS LYKKE. So it was.

NILS STENSSON. Ah, I have it, I have it! I am——

NILS LYKKE. You are Sten Sture's son, good Sir.

NILS STENSSON (with the quiet of amazement). *I* Sten Sture's son!

NILS LYKKE. On the mother's side too your blood is noble. Peter Kanzler spoke not the truth, if he said that a poor peasant woman was your mother.

NILS STENSSON. Oh strange, oh marvellous! —But can I believe——?

NILS LYKKE. You may believe all I tell you. But remember, all this will be merely your ruin, if you should forget what you swore to me by your father's salvation.

NILS STENSSON. Forget it? Nay, that you may be sure I never shall. —But you to whom I have given my word, —tell me—who are you?

NILS LYKKE. My name is Nils Lykke.

NILS STENSSON (surprised). Nils Lykke? Surely not the Danish Councillor?

NILS LYKKE. Even so.

NILS STENSSON. And it was you——? 'Tis strange. How come you——?

NILS LYKKE. ——To be receiving missives from Peter Kanzler? You marvel at that?

NILS STENSSON. I cannot deny it. He has ever named you as our bitterest foe——

NILS LYKKE. And therefore you mistrust me?

NILS STENSSON. Nay, not wholly that; but—well, the devil take musing!

NILS LYKKE. Well said. Go but your own way, and you are as sure of the halter as you are of a Count's title and a chain of gold if you trust to me.

NILS STENSSON. That will I. My hand upon it, dear Sir! Do you but help me with good counsel as long as there is need; when counsel gives place to blows I shall look to myself.

NILS LYKKE. It is well. Come with me now into yonder chamber, and I will tell you how all these matters stand, and what you have still to do.

(Goes out to the right.)

NILS STENSSON (with a glance at the picture). *I* Sten Sture's son! Oh, marvellous as a dream—!

(Goes out after NILS LYKKE.)

ACT FOURTH.

(The Banquet Hall, as before, but without the supper-table.)

(BIORN, the major-domo, enters carrying a lighted branch-candlestick, and lighting in LADY INGER and OLAF SKAKTAVL by the second door, on the left. LADY INGER has a bundle of papers in her hand.)

LADY INGER (to BIORN). And you are sure my daughter spoke with the knight, here in the hall?

BIORN (putting down the branch-candlestick on the table on the left). Sure as may be. I met her even as she stepped into the passage.

LADY INGER. And she seemed greatly moved? Said you not so?

BIORN. She looked all pale and disturbed. I asked if she were sick; she answered not, but said: "Go to mother and tell her the knight sets forth ere daybreak; if she have letters or messages for him, beg her not to delay him needlessly. " And then she added somewhat that I heard not rightly.

LADY INGER. Did you not hear it at all?

BIORN. It sounded to me as though she said: —"I almost fear he has already stayed too long at Ostrat. "

LADY INGER. And the knight? Where is he?

BIORN. In his chamber belike, in the gate-wing.

LADY INGER. It is well. What I have to send by him is ready. Go to him and say I await him here in the hall.

(BIORN goes out to the right.)

OLAF SKAKTAVL. Know you, Lady Inger, —'tis true that in such things I am blind as a mole; yet seems it to me as though—hm!

LADY INGER. Well?

OLAF SKAKTAVL. ——As though Nils Lykke loved your daughter.

LADY INGER. Then it seems you are not so blind after all; I am the more deceived if you be not right. Marked you not at supper how eagerly he listened to the least word I let fall concerning Elina?

OLAF SKAKTAVL. He forgot both food and drink.

LADY INGER. And our secret business as well.

OLAF SKAKTAVL. Ay, and what is more—the papers from Peter Kanzler.

LADY INGER. And from all this you conclude——?

OLAF SKAKTAVL. From all this I chiefly conclude that, as you know Nils Lykke and the name he bears, especially as concerns women——

LADY INGER. ——I should be right glad to know him outside my gates?

OLAF SKAKTAVL. Ay; and that as soon as may be.

LADY INGER (smiling). Nay—the case is just the contrary, Olaf Skaktavl!

OLAF SKAKTAVL. How mean you?

LADY INGER. If things be as we both think, Nils Lykke must in nowise depart from Ostrat yet awhile.

OLAF SKAKTAVL (looks at her with disapproval). Are you beginning on crooked courses again, Lady Inger? What scheme have you now in your mind? Something that may increase your own power at the cost of our——

LADY INGER. Oh this blindness, that makes you all unjust to me! I see well you think I purpose to make Nils Lykke my daughter's husband. Were such a thought in my mind, why had I refused to take part in what is afoot in Sweden, when Nils Lykke and all the Danish crew seem willing to support it?

OLAF SKAKTAVL. Then if it be not your wish to win him and bind him to you—what would you with him?

LADY INGER. I will tell you in few words. In a letter to me, Nils Lykke has spoken of the high fortune it were to be allied to our house; and I do not say but, for a moment, I let myself think of the matter.

OLAF SKAKTAVL. Ay, see you!

LADY INGER. To wed Nils Lykke to one of my house were doubtless a great step toward reconciling many jarring forces in our land.

OLAF SKAKTAVL. Meseems your daughter Merete's marriage with Vinzents Lunge might have taught you the cost of such a step as this. Scarce had my lord gained a firm footing in our midst, when he began to make free with both our goods and our rights——

LADY INGER. I know it even too well, Olaf Skaktavl! But times there be when my thoughts are manifold and strange. I cannot impart them fully either to you or to any one else. Often I know not what were best for me. And yet—a second time to choose a Danish lord for a son-in-law, —nought but the uttermost need could drive me to that resource; and heaven be praised—things have not yet come to that!

OLAF SKAKTAVL. I am no wiser than before, Lady Inger; —why would you keep Nils Lykke at Ostrat?

LADY INGER (softly). Because I owe him an undying hate. Nils Lykke has done me deadlier wrong than any other man. I cannot tell you wherein it lies; but I shall never rest till I am avenged on him. See you not now? Say that Nils Lykke were to love my daughter—as meseems were like enough. I will persuade him to remain here; he shall learn to know Elina well. She is both fair and wise. —Ah if he should one day come before me, with hot love in his heart, to beg for her hand! Then—to chase him away like a hound; to drive him off with jibes and scorn; to make it known over all the land that Nils Lykke had come a-wooing to Ostrat in vain! I tell you I would give ten years of my life but to see that day!

OLAF SKAKTAVL. In faith and truth, Inger Gyldenlove—is this your purpose towards him?

LADY INGER. This and nought else, as sure as God lives! Trust me, Olaf Skaktavl, I mean honestly by my countrymen; but I am in no way my own master. Things there be that must be kept hidden, or 'twere my death-blow. But let me once be safe on *that* side, and you shall see if I have forgotten the oath I swore by Knut Alfson's corpse.

OLAF SKAKTAVL (shakes her by the hand). Thanks for those words! I am loath indeed to think evil of you. —Yet, touching your design towards this knight, methinks 'tis a dangerous game you would play. What if you had misreckoned? What if your daughter— —? 'Tis said no woman can stand against this subtle devil.

LADY INGER. My daughter? Think you that she— —? Nay, have no fear of that; I know Elina better. All she has heard of his renown has but made her hate him the more. You saw with your own eyes— —

OLAF SKAKTAVL. Ay, but—a woman's mind is shifting ground to build on. 'Twere best you looked well before you.

LADY INGER. That will I, be sure; I will watch them narrowly. But even were he to succeed in luring her into his toils, I have but to whisper two words in her ear, and— —

OLAF SKAKTAVL. What then?

LADY INGER. — —She will shrink from him as though he were sent by the foul Tempter himself. Hist, Olaf Skaktavl! Here he comes. Now be cautious.

(NILS LYKKE enters by the foremost door on the right.)

NILS LYKKE (approaches LADY INGER courteously). My noble hostess has summoned me.

LADY INGER. I have learned through my daughter that you are minded to leave us to-night.

NILS LYKKE. Even so, to my sorrow; —since my business at Ostrat is over.

OLAF SKAKTAVL. Not before I have the papers.

NILS LYKKE. True, true. I had well-nigh forgotten the weightiest part of my errand. 'Twas the fault of our noble hostess. With such pleasant skill did she keep her guests in talk at the table— —

LADY INGER. That you no longer remembered what had brought you hither? I rejoice to hear it; For that was my design. Methought that if my guest, Nils Lykke, were to feel at ease in Ostrat, he must forget— —

NILS LYKKE. What, lady?

LADY INGER. — —First of all his errand—and then all that had gone before it.

NILS LYKKE (to OLAF SKAKTAVL, while he takes out the packet and hands it to him). The papers from Peter Kanzler. You will find them a full account of our partizans in Sweden.

OLAF SKAKTAVL. It is well.

(Sits down by the table on the left, where he opens the packet and examines its contents.)

NILS LYKKE. And now, Lady Inger Gyldenlove—I know not that aught remains to keep me here.

LADY INGER. Were it things of state alone that had brought us together, you might be right. But I should be loath to think so.

NILS LYKKE. You would say— —?

LADY INGER. I would say that 'twas not alone as a Danish Councillor or as the ally of Peter Kanzler that Nils Lykke came to be my guest. —Do I err in fancying that somewhat you may have heard down in Denmark may have made you desirous of closer acquaintance with the Lady of Ostrat.

NILS LYKKE. Far be it from me to deny— —

OLAF SKAKTAVL (turning over the papers). Strange. No letter.

NILS LYKKE. ——Lady Inger Gyldenlove's fame is all too widely spread that I should not long have been eager to see her face to face.

LADY INGER. So I thought. But what, then, is an hour's jesting talk at the supper-table? Let us try to sweep away all that has separated us till now; it may well happen that the Nils Lykke I know may wipe out the grudge I bore the one I knew not. Prolong your stay here but a few days, Sir Councillor! I dare not persuade Olaf Skaktavl thereto, since his secret charge in Sweden calls him hence. But as for you, doubtless your sagacity has placed all things beforehand in such train, that your presence can scarce be needed. Trust me, your time shall not pass tediously with us; at least you will find me and my daughter heartily desirous to do all we may to pleasure you.

NILS LYKKE. I doubt neither your goodwill toward me nor your daughter's; of that I have had full proof. And you will doubtless allow that the necessity which calls for my presence elsewhere must be more vital, since, despite your kindness, I must declare my longer stay at Ostrat impossible.

LADY INGER. Is it even so! —Know you, Sir Councillor, were I evilly disposed, I might fancy you had come to Ostrat to try a fall with me, and that, having lost, you like not to linger on the battlefield among the witnesses of your defeat.

NILS LYKKE (smiling). There might be some show of reason for such a reading of the case; but sure it is that as yet *I* hold not the battle lost.

LADY INGER. Be that as it may, it might at any rate be retrieved, if you would tarry some days with us. You see yourself, I am still doubting and wavering at the parting of the ways, —persuading my redoubtable assailant not to quit the field. —Well, to speak plainly, the thing is this: your alliance with the disaffected in Sweden still seems to me somewhat—ay, what shall I call it? — somewhat miraculous, Sir Councillor! I tell you this frankly, dear Sir! The thought that has moved the King's Council to this secret step is in truth most politic; but it is strangely at variance with the deeds of certain of your countrymen in bygone years. Be not offended, then, if my trust in your fair promises needs to be somewhat strengthened ere I can place my whole welfare in your hands.

NILS LYKKE. A longer stay at Ostrat would scarce help towards that end; since I purpose not to make any further effort to shake your resolution.

LADY INGER. Then must I pity you from my heart. Ay, Sir Councillor—'tis true I stand here an unfriended widow; yet may you trust my word when I prophesy that this visit to Ostrat will strew your future path with thorns.

NILS LYKKE (with a smile). Is that your prophecy, Lady Inger?

LADY INGER. Truly it is! What can one say dear Sir? 'Tis a calumnious age. Many a scurril knave will make scornful rhymes concerning you. Ere half a year is out, you will be all men's fable; people will stop and gaze after you on the high roads; 'twill be: "Look, look; there rides Sir Nils Lykke, that fared north to Ostrat to trap Inger Gyldenlove, and was caught in his own nets. "—Nay nay, why so impatient, Sir Knight! 'Tis not that *I* think so; I do but forecast the thought of the malicious and evil-minded; and of them, alas! there are many. —Ay, 'tis shame; but so it is—you will reap nought but mockery—mockery, because a woman was craftier than you. "Like a cunning fox, " men will say, "he crept into Ostrat; like a beaten hound he slunk away. " —And one thing more: think you not that Peter Kanzler and his friends will forswear your alliance, when 'tis known that I venture not to fight under a standard borne by you?

NILS LYKKE. You speak wisely, lady! And so, to save myself from mockery—and further, to avoid breaking with all our dear friends in Sweden—I must needs——

LADY INGER (hastily). ——prolong your stay at Ostrat?

OLAF SKAKTAVL (who has been listening). He is in the trap!

NILS LYKKE. No, my noble lady; —I must needs bring you to terms within this hour.

LADY INGER. But what if you should fail?

NILS LYKKE. I shall *not* fail.

LADY INGER. You lack not confidence, it seems.

NILS LYKKE. What shall we wager that you make not common cause with myself and Peter Kanzler?

LADY INGER. Ostrat Castle against your knee-buckles.

NILS LYKKE (points to himself and cries:) Olaf Skaktavl—here stands the master of Ostrat!

LADY INGER. Sir Councillor— —!

NILS LYKKE (to LADY INGER). I accept not the wager; for in a moment you will gladly give Ostrat Castle, and more to boot, to be freed from the snare wherein not I but you are tangled.

LADY INGER. Your jest, Sir, grows a vastly merry one.

NILS LYKKE. 'Twill be merrier yet—at least for me. You boast that you have overreached me. You threaten to heap on me all men's scorn and mockery. Ah, beware that you stir not up my vengefulness; For with two words I can bring you to your knees at my feet.

LADY INGER. Ha-ha— — — —! (Stops suddenly, as if struck by a foreboding.) And the two words, Nils Lykke? —the two words— —?

NILS LYKKE. — —The secret of Sten Sture's son and yours.

LADY INGER (with a shriek). Oh, Jesus Christ— —!

OLAF SKAKTAVL. Inger Gyldenlove's son! What say you?

LADY INGER (half kneeling to NILS LYKKE). Mercy! oh be merciful — —!

NILS LYKKE (raises her up). Collect yourself, and let us talk calmly.

LADY INGER (in a low voice, as though bewildered). Did you hear it, Olaf Skaktavl? or was it but a dream? Heard you what he said?

NILS LYKKE. It was no dream, Lady Inger!

LADY INGER. And you know it! You, —you! — Where is he then? Where have you got him? What would you do with him? (Screams.)

Do not kill him, Nils Lykke! Give him back to me! Do not kill my child!

OLAF SKAKTAVL. Ah, I begin to understand— —

LADY INGER. And this fear— —this torturing dread! Through all these years it has been ever with me— — — — and then all fails at last, and I must bear this agony! —Oh Lord my God, is it right of thee? Was it for this thou gavest him to me? (Controls herself and says with forced composure:) Nils Lykke—tell me *one* thing. Where have you got him? Where is he?

NILS LYKKE. With his foster-father.

LADY INGER. Still with his foster-father. Oh, that merciless man— —! For ever to deny my prayers. —But it *must* not go on thus! Help me, Olaf Skaktavl!

OLAF SKAKTAVL. I?

NILS LYKKE. There will be no need, if only you— —

LADY INGER. Hearken, Sir Councillor! What you know you shall know thoroughly. And you too, my old and faithful friend— —! Listen then. To-night you bade me call to mind that fatal day when Knut Alfson was slain at Oslo. You bade me remember the promise I made as I stood by his corpse amid the bravest men in Norway. I was scarce full-grown then; but I felt God's strength in me, and methought, as many have thought since, that the Lord himself had set his mark on me and chosen me to fight in the forefront for my country's cause. Was it vanity? Or was it a calling from on high? That I have never clearly known. But woe to him that has a great mission laid upon him. For seven years I fear not to say that I kept my promise faithfully. I stood by my countrymen in all their miseries. All my playmates were now wives and mothers. I alone could give ear to no wooer—not to one. That you know best, Olaf Skaktavl! Then I saw Sten Sture for the first time. Fairer man had never met my sight.

NILS LYKKE. Ah, now it grows clear to me! Sten Sture was then in Norway on a secret errand. We Danes were not to know that he wished your friends well.

LADY INGER. Disguised as a mean serving-man he lived a whole winter under one roof with me. That winter I thought less and less of the country's weal— — — —. So fair a man had I never seen, and I had lived well-nigh five-and-twenty years. Next autumn Sten Sture came once more; and when he departed again he took with him, in all secrecy, a little child. "Twas not folk's evil tongues I feared; but our cause would have suffered had it got about the Sten Sture stood so near to me. The child was given to Peter Kanzler to rear. I waited for better times, that were soon to come. They never came. Sten Sture took a wife two years later in Sweden, and, dying, left a widow— —

OLAF SKAKTAVL. — —And with her a lawful heir to his name and rights.

LADY INGER. Time after time I wrote to Peter Kanzler and besought him to give me back my child. But he was ever deaf to my prayers. "Cast in your lot with us once for all, " he said, "and I send your son back to Norway; not before. " But 'twas even that I dared not do. We of the disaffected party were then ill regarded by many timorous folk. If these had got tidings of how things stood—oh, I know it! —to cripple the mother they had gladly meted to the child the fate that would have been King Christiern's had he not saved himself by flight. [1] But besides that, the Danes were active. They spared neither threats nor promises to force me to join them.

OLAF SKAKTAVL. 'Twas but reason. The eyes of all men were fixed on you as the vane that should show them how to shape their course.

LADY INGER. Then came Herlof Hyttefad's revolt. Do you remember that time, Olaf Skaktavl? Was it not as though the whole land was filled with the sunlight of a new spring. Mighty voices summoned me to come forth; —yet I dared not. I stood doubting—far from the strife—in my lonely castle. At times it seemed as though the Lord God himself were calling me; but then would come the killing dread again to paralyse my will. "Who will win? " that was the question that was ever ringing in my ears. 'Twas but a short spring that had come to Norway. Herlof Hyttefad, and many more with him, were broken on the wheel during the months that followed. None could call me to account; yet there lacked not covert threats from Denmark. What if they knew the secret? At last methought they must know; I knew not how else to understand their words. 'Twas even in that time of agony that Gyldenlove the High Steward, came hither and sought me in marriage. Let any mother that has feared for her child think herself in my place! —and homeless in the hearts of my countrymen. Then came the quiet years. There was now no whisper of revolt. Our masters might grind us down even as heavily as they listed. There were times when I loathed myself. What had I to do? Nought but to endure terror and scorn and bring forth daughters into the world. My daughters! God forgive me if I have had no mother's heart towards them. My wifely duties were as serfdom to me; how then could I love my daughters? Oh, how different with my son! *He* was the child of my very soul. He was the one thing that brought to mind the time when I was a woman and nought but a woman—and him they had taken from me! He was growing up among strangers, who might sow in him the seed of destruction! Olaf Skaktavl—had I wandered like you on the lonely hills, hunted and forsaken, in winter and storm—if I had but held my child in my arms, —trust me, I had not sorrowed and wept so sore as I have sorrowed and wept for him from his birth even to this hour.

OLAF SKAKTAVL. There is my hand. I have judged you too hardly, Lady Inger! Command me even as before; I will obey. —Ay, by all the saints, I know what it is to sorrow for a child.

LADY INGER. Yours was slain by bloody men. But what is death to the restless terror of all these long years?

NILS LYKKE. Mark, then—'tis in your power to end this terror. You have but to reconcile the opposing parties, and neither will think of seizing on your child as a pledge of your faith.

LADY INGER (to herself). This is the vengeance of Heaven. (Looks at him.) In one word, what do you demand?

NILS LYKKE. I demand first that you shall call the people of the northern districts to arms, in support of the disaffected in Sweden.

LADY INGER. And next— —?

NILS LYKKE. — —that you do your best to advance young Count Sture's ancestral claim to the throne of Sweden.

LADY INGER. His? You demand that I— —?

OLAF SKAKTAVL (softly). It is the wish of many Swedes, and 'twould serve our turn too.

NILS LYKKE. You hesitate, lady? You tremble for your son's safety. What better can you wish than to see his half-brother on the throne?

LADY INGER (in thought). True—true——

NILS LYKKE (looks at her sharply). Unless there be other plans afoot——

LADY INGER. What mean you?

NILS LYKKE. Inger Gyldenlove might have a mind to be a—a kings mother.

LADY INGER. No, no! Give me back my child, and let who will have the crowns. But know you so surely that Count Sture is willing——?

NILS LYKKE. Of that he will himself assure you.

LADY INGER. Himself?

NILS LYKKE. Even now.

OLAF SKAKTAVL. How now?

LADY INGER. What say you?

NILS LYKKE. In one word, Count Sture is in Ostrat.

OLAF SKAKTAVL. Here?

NILS LYKKE (to LADY INGER). You have doubtless been told that another rode through the gate along with me? The Count was my attendant.

LADY INGER (softly). I am in his power. I have no longer any choice. (Looks at him and says:) 'Tis well, Sir Councillor—I will assure you of my support.

NILS LYKKE. In writing?

LADY INGER. As you will.

(Goes to the table on the left, sits down, and takes writing materials from the drawer.)

NILS LYKKE (aside, standing by the table on the right). At last, then, I win!

LADY INGER (after a moment's thought, turns suddenly in her chair to OLAF SKAKTAVL and whispers). Olaf Skaktavl—I am certain of it now—Nils Lykke is a traitor!

OLAF SKAKTAVL (softly). What? You think——?

LADY INGER. He has treachery in his heart

(Lays the paper before her and dips the pen in the ink.)

OLAF SKAKTAVL. And yet you would give him a written promise that may be your ruin?

LADY INGER. Hush; leave me to act. Nay, wait and listen first——

(Talks with him in a whisper.)

NILS LYKKE (softly, watching them). Ah, take counsel together as much as ye list! All danger is over now. With her written consent in my pocket, I can denounce her when I please. A secret message to Jens Bielke this very night. —I tell him but the truth— that the young Count Sture is not at Ostrat. And then to-morrow, when the road is open—to Trondhiem with my young friend, and thence by ship to Copenhagen with him as my prisoner. Once we have him safe in the castle-tower, we can dictate to Lady Inger what terms we will. And I——? Methinks after this the King will scarce place the French mission in other hands than mine.

LADY INGER (still whispering to OLAF SKAKTAVL). Well, you understand me?

OLAF SKAKTAVL. Ay, fully. Let us risk it.

(Goes out by the back, to the right. NILS STENSSON comes in by the first door on the right, unseen by LADY INGER, who has begun to write.)

NILS STENSSON (in a low voice). Sir Knight, —Sir Knight!

NILS LYKKE (moves towards him). Rash boy! What would you here? Said I not you were to wait within until I called you?

NILS STENSSON. How could I? Now you have told me that Inger Gyldenlove is my mother, I thirst more than ever to see her face to face— — Oh, it is she! How proud and lofty she seems! Even thus did I ever picture her. Fear not, dear Sir, I shall do nought rashly. Since I have learnt this secret, I feel, as it were, older and wiser. I will no longer be wild and heedless; I will be even as other well-born youths. —Tell me, —knows she that I am here? Surely you have prepared her?

NILS LYKKE. Ay, sure enough; but— —

NILS STENSSON. Well?

NILS LYKKE. — —She will not own you for her son.

NILS STENSSON. Will not own me? But she *is* my mother. —Oh, if there be no other way—(takes out a ring which he wears on a cord round his neck)—show her this ring. I have worn it since my earliest childhood; she must surely know its history.

NILS LYKKE. Hide the ring, man! Hide it, I say! You mistake me. Lady Inger doubts not at all that you are her child; but—ay, look about you; look at all this wealth; look at these mighty ancestors and kinsmen whose pictures deck the walls both high and low; look lastly at herself, the haughty dame, used to bear sway as the first noblewoman in the kingdom. Think you it can be to her mind to take a poor ignorant youth by the hand before all men's eyes and say: Behold my son!

NILS STENSSON. Ay, you are right, I am poor and ignorant. I have nought to offer her in return for what I crave. Oh, never have I felt my poverty weigh on me till this hour! But tell me— what think you I should do to win her love? Tell me, dear Sir; sure you must know.

NILS LYKKE. You must win your father's kingdom. But until that may be, look well that you wound not her ears by hinting at kinship or the like. She will bear her as though she believed you to be the real Count Sture, until you have made yourself worthy to be called her son.

NILS STENSSON. Oh, but tell me— —!

NILS LYKKE. Hush; hush!

LADY INGER (rises and hands him a paper). Sir Knight—here is my promise.

NILS LYKKE. I thank you.

LADY INGER (notices NILS STENSSON). Ah, —this young man is— —?

NILS LYKKE. Ay, Lady Inger, he is Count Sture.

LADY INGER (aside, looks at him stealthily). Feature for feature; —ay, by God, —it is Sten Sture's son! (Approaches him and says with cold courtesy.) I bid you welcome under my roof, Count! It rests with you whether or not we shall bless this meeting a year hence.

NILS STENSSON. With me? Oh, do but tell me what I must do! Trust me, I have courage and good-will enough— —

NILS LYKKE (listens uneasily). What is this noise and uproar, Lady Inger? There are people pressing hitherward. What does this mean?

LADY INGER (in a loud voice). 'Tis the spirits awaking!

(OLAF SKAKTAVL, EINAR HUK, BIORN, FINN, and a number of Peasants and Retainers come in from the back, on the right.)

THE PEASANTS AND RETAINERS. Hail to Lady Inger Gyldenlove!

LADY INGER (to OLAF SKAKTAVL). Have you told them what is in hand?

OLAF SKAKTAVL. I have told them all they need to know.

LADY INGER (to the Crowd). Ay, now, my faithful house-folk and peasants, now must ye arm you as best you can and will. What I forbade you to-night you have now my fullest leave to do. And here I present to you the young Count Sture, the coming ruler of Sweden—and Norway too, if God will it so.

THE WHOLE CROWD. Hail to him! Hail to Count Sture!

(General excitement. The Peasants and Retainers choose out weapons and put on breastplates and helmets, amid great noise.)

NILS LYKKE (softly and uneasily). The spirits awaking, she said? I but feigned to conjure up the devil of revolt—'twere a cursed spite if he got the upper hand of us.

LADY INGER (to NILS STENSSON). Here I give you the first earnest of our service—thirty mounted men, to follow you as bodyguard. Trust me—ere you reach the frontier many hundreds will have ranged themselves under my banner and yours. Go, then, and God be with you!

NILS STENSSON. Thanks, —Inger Gyldenlove! Thanks—and be sure that you shall never have cause to shame you for—for Count Sture! If you see me again I shall have won my father's kingdom.

NILS LYKKE (to himself). Ay, *if* she see you again!

OLAF SKAKTAVL. The horses wait, good fellows! Are ye ready?

THE PEASANTS. Ay, ay, ay!

NILS LYKKE (uneasily, to LADY INGER). What? You mean not to-night, even now——?

LADY INGER. This very moment, Sir Knight!

NILS LYKKE. Nay, nay, impossible!

LADY INGER. I have said it.

NILS LYKKE (softly, to NILS STENSSON). Obey her not!

NILS STENSSON. How can I otherwise? I *will*; I *must!*

NILS LYKKE (with authority). And *me!*

NILS STENSSON. I shall keep my word; be sure of that. The secret shall not pass my lips till you yourself release me. But she is my mother!

NILS LYKKE (aside). And Jens Bielke in wait on the road! Damnation! He will snatch the prize out of my fingers— — (To LADY INGER.) Wait till to-morrow!

LADY INGER (to NILS STENSSON). Count Sture—do you obey me or not?

NILS STENSSON. To horse! (Goes up towards the background).

NILS LYKKE (aside). Unhappy boy! He knows not what he does. (To LADY INGER.) Well, since so it must be, —farewell!

(Bows hastily, and begins to move away.)

LADY INGER (detains him). Nay, stay! Not so, Sir Knight, — not so!

NILS LYKKE. What mean you?

LADY INGER (in a low voice). Nils Lykke—you are a traitor! Hush! Let no one see there is dissension in the camp of the leaders. You have won Peter Kanzler's trust by some devilish cunning that as yet I see not through. You have forced me to rebellious acts—not to help our cause, but to further your own plots, whatever they may be. I can draw back no more. But think not therefore that you have conquered! I shall contrive to make you harmless— —

NILS LYKKE (lays his hand involuntarily on his sword). Lady Inger!

LADY INGER. Be calm, Sir Councillor! Your life is safe. But you come not outside the gates of Ostrat before victory is ours.

NILS LYKKE. Death and destruction!

LADY INGER. It boots not to resist. You come not from this place. So rest you quiet; 'tis your wisest course.

NILS LYKKE (to himself). Ah, —I am overreached. She has been craftier than I. (A thought strikes him.) But if I yet— —?

LADY INGER (to OLAF SKAKTAVL). Ride with Count Sture's troops to the frontier; then without pause to Peter Kanzler, and bring me back my child. Now has he no longer any plea for keeping from me what is my own. (Adds, as OLAF SKAKTAVL is going:) Wait; a token. —He that wears Sten Sture's ring is my son.

OLAF SKAKTAVL. By all the saints, you shall have him!

LADY INGER. Thanks, —thanks, my faithful friend!

NILS LYKKE (to FINN, whom he has beckoned to him unobserved, and with whom he has been whispering). Good—now manage to slip out. Let none see you. The Swedes are in ambush two miles hence. Tell the commander that Count Sture is dead. The young man you see there must not be touched. Tell the commander so. Tell him the boy's life is worth thousands to me.

FINN. It shall be done.

LADY INGER (who has meanwhile been watching NILS LYKKE). And now go, all of you; go with God! (Points to NILS LYKKE.) This noble knight cannot find it in his heart to leave his friends at Ostrat so hastily. He will abide here with me till the tidings of your victory arrive.

NILS LYKKE (to himself). Devil!

NILS STENSSON (seizes his hand). Trust me—you shall not have long to wait!

NILS LYKKE. It is well; it is well! (Aside.) All may yet be saved. If only my message reach Jens Bielke in time— —

LADY INGER (to EINAR HUK, the bailiff, pointing to FINN). And let that man be placed under close guard in the castle dungeon.

FINN. Me?

THE BAILIFF AND THE SERVANTS. Finn!

NILS LYKKE (aside). My last anchor gone!

LADY INGER (imperatively). To the dungeon with him!

(EINAR HUK, BIORN, and a couple of the house-servants lead FINN out to the left.)

ALL THE REST (except NILS LYKKE, rushing out to the right). Away! To horse, —to horse! Hail to Lady Inger Gyldenlove!

LADY INGER (passes close to NILS LYKKE as she follows the others). Who wins?

NILS LYKKE (remains alone). Who? Ay, woe to you; —your victory will cost you dear. *I* wash my hands of it. 'Tis not *I* that am murdering him. But my prey is escaping me none the less; and the revolt will grow and spread! —Ah, 'tis a foolhardy, a frantic game I have been playing here! (Listens at the window.) There they go clattering out through the gateway. —Now 'tis closed after them—and I am left here a prisoner. No way of escape! Within half-an-hour the Swedes will be upon him. 'Twill be life or death. But if they should take him alive after all? —Were I but free, I could overtake the Swedes ere they reach the frontier, and make them deliver him up. (Goes towards the window in the background and looks out.) Damnation! Guards outside on every hand. Can there be no way out of this? (Comes quickly forward again; suddenly stops and listens.) What is that? Music and singing. It seems to come from Elina's chamber. Ay, it is she that is singing. Then she is still awake—— (A thought seems to strike him.) Elina! —Ah, if *that* could be! If it could but——And why should I not? Am I not still myself? Says not the song: —

Fair maidens a-many they sigh and they pine;
"Ah God, that Nils Lykke were mine, mine, mine. "

And she——? —— ——Elina Gyldenlove shall set me free!

(Goes quickly but stealthily towards the first door on the left.)

NOTES.

[1] King Christian II. of Denmark (the perpetrator of the massacre at Stockholm known as the Blood-Bath) fled to Holland in 1523, five

years before the date assigned to this play, in order to escape death or imprisonment at the hands of his rebellious nobles, who summoned his uncle, Frederick I., to the throne. Returning to Denmark in 1532, Christian was thrown into prison, where he spent the last twenty-seven years of his life.

ACT FIFTH.

(The Banquet Hall. It is still night. The hall is but dimly lighted by a branch-candlestick on the table, in front, on the right.)

(LADY INGER is sitting by the table, deep in thought.)

LADY INGER (after a pause). They call me keen-witted beyond all others in the land. I believe they are right. The keenest- witted—— No one knows how I became so. For more than twenty years I have fought to save my child. *That* is the key to the riddle. Ay, that sharpens the wits! My wits? Where have they flown to-night? What has become of my forethought? There is a ringing and rushing in my ears. I see shapes before me, so life-like that methinks I could lay hold on them. (Springs up.) Lord Jesus—what is this? Am I no longer mistress of my reason? Is it to come to that——? (Presses her clasped hands over her head; sits down again, and says more calmly:) Nay, 'tis nought. It will pass. There is no fear; —it will pass. How peaceful it is in the hall to-night! No threatening looks from forefathers or kinsfolk. No need to turn their faces to the wall. (Rises again.) Ay, 'twas well that I took heart at last. We shall conquer; —and then I am at the end of my longings. I shall have my child again. (Takes up the light as if to go, but stops and says musingly:) At the end? The end? To get him back? Is that all? —is there nought further? (Sets the light down on the table.) That heedless word that Nils Lykke threw forth at random—— How could he see my unborn thought? (More softly.) A king's mother? A king's mother, he said——Why not? Have not my forefathers ruled as kings, even though they bore not the kingly name? Has not *my* son as good a title as the other to the rights of the house of Sture? In the sight of God he has—if so be there is justice in Heaven. And in an hour of terror I have signed away his rights. I have recklessly squandered them, as a ransom for his freedom. If they could be recovered? —Would Heaven be angered, if I——? Would it call down fresh troubles on my head if I were to——? Who knows; who knows! It may be safest to refrain. (Takes up the light again.) I shall have my child again. *That* must suffice me. I will try to rest. All these desperate thoughts, —I will sleep them away. (Goes towards the back, but stops in the middle of the hall, and says broodingly:) A king's mother!

(Goes slowly out at the back, to the left.)

(After a short pause, NILS LYKKE and ELINA GYLDENLOVE enter noiselessly by the first door on the left. NILS LYKKE has a small lantern in his hand.)

NILS LYKKE. (throws the light from his lantern around, so as to search the room). All is still. I must begone.

ELINA. Oh, let me look but once more into your eyes, before you leave me.

NILS LYKKE (embraces her). Elina!

ELINA (after a short pause). Will you come nevermore to Ostrat?

NILS LYKKE. How can you doubt that I will come? Are you not henceforth my betrothed? —But will *you* be true to *me,* Elina? Will you not forget me ere we meet again?

ELINA. Do you ask if I *will* be true? Have I any will left then? Have I power to be untrue to you, even if I would? —you came by night; you knocked upon my door; —and I opened to you. You spoke to me. What was it you said? You gazed in my eyes. What was the mystic might that turned my brain and lured me, as it were, within a magic net? (Hides her face on his shoulder.) Oh, look not on me, Nils Lykke! You must not look upon me after this—— True, say you? Do you not own me? I am yours; —I must be yours—to all eternity.

NILS LYKKE. Now, by my knightly honour, ere the year be past, you shall sit as my wife in the hall of my fathers.

ELINA. No vows, Nils Lykke! No oaths to me.

NILS LYKKE. What mean you? Why do you shake your head so mournfully?

ELINA. Because I know that the same soft words wherewith you turned my brain, you have whispered to so many a one before. Nay, nay, be not angry, my beloved! In nought do I reproach you, as I did while yet I knew you not. Now I understand how high above all others is your goal. How can love be aught to you but a pastime, or woman but a toy?

NILS LYKKE. Elina, —hear me!

ELINA. As I grew up, your name was ever in my ears. I hated the name, for meseemed that all women were dishonoured by your life. And yet, —how strange! —when I built up in my dreams the life that should be mine, you were ever my hero, though I knew it not. Now I understand it all—now know I what it was I felt. It was a foreboding, a mysterious longing for you, you only one— for you that were one day to come and glorify my life.

NILS LYKKE (aside, putting down the lantern on the table). How is it with me? This dizzy fascination— — If this it be to love, then have I never known it till this hour. —Is there not yet time — —? Oh horror—Lucia!

(Sinks into a chair.)

ELINA. What ails you? So heavy a sigh— —

NILS LYKKE. O, 'tis nought, —nought! Elina, —now will I confess all to you. I have have beguiled many with both words and glances; I have said to many a one what I whispered to you this night. But trust me— —

ELINA. Hush! No more of that. My love is no exchange for that you give me. No, no; I love you because your every glance commands it like a king's decree. (Lies down at his feet.) Oh, let me once more stamp that kingly message deep into my soul, though well I know it stands imprinted there for all time and eternity. Dear God—how little I have known myself! 'Twas but to-night I said to my mother: "My pride is my life. " And what is my pride? Is it to know that my countrymen are free, or that my house is held in honour throughout the lands? Oh, no, no! My love is my pride. The little dog is proud when he may sit by his master's feet and eat bread-crumbs from his hand. Even so am I proud, so long as I may sit at your feet, while your looks and your words nourish me with the bread of life. See, therefore, I say to you, even as I said but now to my mother: "My love is my life; " for therein lies all my pride, now and evermore.

NILS LYKKE (raises her up on his lap). Nay, nay—not at my feet, but at my side is your place, —should fate set me never so high. Ay, Elina—you have led me into a better path; and if it be granted me some day to atone by a deed of fame for the sins of my reckless youth, the honour shall be yours as well as mine.

ELINA. Ah, you speak as though I were still the Elina that but this evening flung down the flowers at your feet. I have read in my books of the many-coloured life in far-off lands. To the winding of horns the knight rides forth into the greenwood, with his falcon on his wrist. Even so do you go your way through life; —your name rings out before you whithersoever you fare. —All that I desire of your glory, is to rest like the falcon on your arm. I too was blind as he to light and life, till you loosed the hood from my eyes and set me soaring high over the leafy tree- tops; —But, trust me—bold as my flight may be, yet shall I ever turn back to my cage.

NILS LYKKE (rises). Then I bid defiance to the past! See now; — take this ring, and be *mine* before God and men—*mine,* ay, though it should trouble the dreams of the dead.

ELINA. You make me afraid. What is it that— —?

NILS LYKKE. It is nought. Come, let me place the ring on your finger. —Even so—now are you my betrothed!

ELINA. *I* Nils Lykke's bride! It seems but a dream, all that has befallen this night. Oh, but so fair a dream! My breast is so light. No longer is there bitterness and hatred in my soul. I will atone to all whom I have wronged. I have been unloving to my mother. To-morrow will I go to her; she must forgive me my offence.

NILS LYKKE. And give her consent to our bond.

ELINA. That will she. Oh, I am sure she will. My mother is kind; all the world is kind; —I can feel hatred no more for any living soul—save *one.*

NILS LYKKE. Save *one?*

ELINA. Ah, it is a mournful history. I had a sister— —

NILS LYKKE. Lucia?

ELINA. Have you known Lucia?

NILS LYKKE. No, no; I have but heard her name.

ELINA. She too gave her heart to a knight. He betrayed her; — and now she is in Heaven.

NILS LYKKE. And you— —?

ELINA. I hate him.

NILS LYKKE. Hate him not! If there be mercy in your heart, forgive him his sin. Trust me, he bears his punishment in his own breast.

ELINA. Him I will never forgive! I *cannot*, even if I would; for I have sworn so dear an oath— — (Listening.) Hush! Can you hear— —?

NILS LYKKE. What? Where?

ELINA. Without; far off. The noise of many horsemen on the high-road.

NILS LYKKE. Ah, it is they! And I had forgotten— —! They are coming hither. Then is the danger great; —I must begone!

ELINA. But whither? Oh, Nils Lykke, what are you hiding— —?

NILS LYKKE. To-morrow, Elina— —; for as God lives, I will return then. —Quickly now—where is the secret passage you told me of?

ELINA. Through the grave-vault. See, —here is the trap-door.

NILS LYKKE. The grave-vault! (To himself.) No matter, he *must* be saved!

ELINA (by the window). The horsemen have reached the gate— —

(Hands him the lantern.)

NILS LYKKE. Well, now I go— —

(Begins to descend.)

ELINA. Go forward along the passage till you reach the coffin with the death's-head and the black cross; it is Lucia's— —

NILS LYKKE (climbs back hastily and shuts the trap-door to). Lucia's! Pah——!

ELINA. What said you?

NILS LYKKE. Nay, nought. It was the scent of the grave that made me dizzy.

ELINA. Hark; they are hammering at the gate!

NILS LYKKE (lets the lantern fall). Ah! too late——!

(BIORN enters hurriedly from the right, carrying a light.)

ELINA (goes towards him). What is amiss, Biorn? What is it?

BIORN. An ambuscade! Count Sture——

ELINA. Count Sture? What of him?

NILS LYKKE. Have they killed him?

BIORN (to ELINA). Where is your mother?

TWO HOUSE-SERVANTS (rushing in from the right). Lady Inger! Lady Inger!

(LADY INGER GYLDENLOVE enters by the first door on the left, with a branch-candlestick, lighted, in her hand, and says quickly:)

LADY INGER. I know all. Down with you to the courtyard! Keep the gate open for our friends, but closed against all others!

(Puts down the candlestick on the table to the left. BIORN and the two House-Servants go out again to the right.)

LADY INGER (to NILS LYKKE). So *that* was the trap, Sir Councillor!

NILS LYKKE. Inger Gyldenlove, trust me——!

LADY INGER. An ambuscade that was to snap him up, as soon as you had got the promise that should destroy me!

NILS LYKKE (takes out the paper and tears it to pieces). There is your promise. I keep nothing that can bear witness against you.

LADY INGER. What will you do?

NILS LYKKE. From this hour I am your champion. If I have sinned against you, —by Heaven I will strive to repair my crime. But now I *must* out, if I have to hew my way through the gate! —Elina— tell your mother all! —And you, Lady Inger, let our reckoning be forgotten! Be generous—and silent! Trust me, ere the day dawns you shall owe me a life's gratitude.

(Goes out quickly to the right.)

LADY INGER (looks after him with exultation). It is well! I understand him! (Turns to ELINA.) Nils Lykke——? Well——?

ELINA. He knocked upon my door, and set this ring upon my finger.

LADY INGER. And he loves you with all his heart?

ELINA. My mother—you are so strange. Oh, ay—I know—it is my unloving ways that have angered you.

LADY INGER. Not so, dear Elina! You are an obedient child. You have opened your door to him; you have hearkened to his soft words. I know full well what it must have cost you for I know your hatred——

ELINA. But, my mother——

LADY INGER. Hush! We have played into each other's hands. What wiles did you use, my subtle daughter? I saw the love shine out of his eyes. Hold him fast now! Draw the net closer and closer about him, and then—— Ah, Elina, if we could but rend his perjured heart within his breast!

ELINA. Woe is me—what is it you say?

LADY INGER. Let not your courage fail you. Hearken to me. I know a word that will keep you firm. Know then—— (Listening.) They are fighting outside the gate. Courage! Now comes the pinch! (Turns again to ELINA.) Know then, Nils Lykke was the man that brought your sister to her grave.

ELINA (with a shriek). Lucia!

LADY INGER. He it was, as truly as there is an Avenger above us!

ELINA. Then Heaven be with me!

LADY INGER (appalled). Elina— —?!

ELINA. I am his bride in the sight of God.

LADY INGER. Unhappy child, —what have you done?

ELINA (in a toneless voice). Made shipwreck of my soul. —Good-night, my mother!

(She goes out to the left.)

LADY INGER. Ha-ha-ha! It goes down-hill now with Inger Gyldenlove's house. There went the last of my daughters. Why could I not keep silence? Had she known nought, it may be she had been happy—after a kind. It *was* to be so. It is written up there in the stars that I am to break off one green branch after another, till the trunk stand leafless at last. 'Tis well, 'tis well! I am to have my son again. Of the others, of my daughters, I will not think. My reckoning? To face my reckoning? —It falls not due till the last great day of wrath. —*That* comes not yet awhile.

NILS STENSSON (calling from outside on the right). Ho—shut the gate!

LADY INGER. Count Sture's voice— —!

NILS STENSSON (rushes in, unarmed, and with his clothes torn, and shouts with a desperate laugh). Well met again, Inger Gyldenlove!

LADY INGER. What have you lost?

NILS STENSSON. My kingdom and my life!

LADY INGER. And the peasants? My servants? —where are they?

NILS STENSSON. You will find the carcasses along the highway. Who has the rest, I know not.

OLAF SKAKTAVL (outside on the right). Count Sture! Where are you?

NILS STENSSON. Here, here!

(OLAF SKAKTAVL comes in with his right hand wrapped in a cloth).

LADY INGER. Alas Olaf Skaktavl, you too——!

OLAF SKAKTAVL. It was impossible to break through.

LADY INGER. You are wounded, I see!

OLAF SKAKTAVL. A finger the less; that is all.

NILS STENSSON. Where are the Swedes?

OLAF SKAKTAVL. At our heels. They are breaking open the gate——

NILS STENSSON. Oh, Jesus! No, no! I *cannot*—I *will* not die.

OLAF SKAKTAVL. A hiding-place, Lady Inger! Is there no corner where we can hide him?

LADY INGER. But if they search the castle——?

NILS STENSSON. Ay, ay; they will find me! And then to be dragged to prison, or strung up——! Oh no, Inger Gyldenlove, — I know full well, —you will never suffer that to be!

OLAF SKAKTAVL (listening). There burst the lock.

LADY INGER (at the window). Many men rush in at the gateway.

NILS STENSSON. And to lose my life *now!* Now, when my true life was but beginning! Now, when I have so lately learnt that I have aught to live for. No, no, no! —Think not I am a coward. Might I but have time to show— —

LADY INGER. I hear them now in the hall below. (Firmly to OLAF SKAKTAVL.) He *must* be saved—cost what it will!

NILS STENSSON (seizes her hand). Oh, I knew it; —you are noble and good!

OLAF SKAKTAVL. But how? Since we cannot hide him— —

NILS STENSSON. Ah, I have it! I have it! The secret— —!

LADY INGER. The secret?

NILS STENSSON. Even so; yours and mine!

LADY INGER. Christ in Heaven—you know it?

NILS STENSSON. From first to last. And now when 'tis life or death— — Where is Nils Lykke?

LADY INGER. Fled.

NILS STENSSON. Fled? Then God help me; for he only can unseal my lips. —But what is a promise against a life! When the Swedish captain comes— —

LADY INGER. What then? What will you do?

NILS STENSSON. Purchase life and freedom; —tell him all.

LADY INGER. Oh no, no; —be merciful!

NILS STENSSON. Nought else can save me. When I have told him what I know— —

LADY INGER (looks at him with suppressed excitement). You will be safe?

NILS STENSSON. Ay, safe! Nils Lykke will speak for me. You see, 'tis the last resource.

LADY INGER (composedly, with emphasis). The last resource? Right, right—the last resource stands open to all. (Points to the left.) See, meanwhile you can hide in there.

NILS STENSSON (softly). Trust me—you will never repent of this.

LADY INGER (half to herself). God grant that you speak the truth!

(NILS STENSSON goes out hastily by the furthest door on the left. OLAF SKAKTAVL is following; but LADY INGER detains him.)

LADY INGER. Did you understand his meaning?

OLAF SKAKTAVL. The dastard! He would betray your secret. He would sacrifice your son to save himself.

LADY INGER. When life is at stake, he said, we must try the last resource. —It is well, Olaf Skaktavl, —let it be as he has said!

OLAF SKAKTAVL. What mean you?

LADY INGER. Life for life! One of them must perish.

OLAF SKAKTAVL. Ah—you would——?

LADY INGER. If we close not the lips of him that is within ere he come to speech with the Swedish captain, then is my son lost to me. But if he be swept from my path, when the time comes I can claim all his rights for my own child. Then shall you see that Inger Ottisdaughter has metal in her yet. And be assured you shall not have long to wait for the vengeance you have thirsted after for twenty years. —Hark! They are coming up the stairs! Olaf Skaktavl, —it lies with you whether to-morrow I shall be a childless woman, or——

OLAF SKAKTAVL. So be it! I have one sound hand left yet. (Gives her his hand.) Inger Gyldenlove—your name shall not die out through me.

(Follows NILS STENSSON into the inner room.)

LADY INGER (pale and trembling). But dare I——? (A noise is heard in the room; she rushes with a scream towards the door.) No, no, —it must not be! (A heavy fall is heard within; she covers her ears with her hands and hurries back across the hall with a wild look. After a pause she takes her hands cautiously away, listens again and says softly:) Now it is over. All is still within— — Thou sawest it, God—I repented me! But Olaf Skaktavl was too swift of hand.

(OLAF SKAKTAVL comes silently into the hall.)

LADY INGER (after a pause, without looking at him). Is it done?

OLAF SKAKTAVL. You need fear him no more; he will betray no one.

LADY INGER (as before). Then he is dumb?

OLAF SKAKTAVL. Six inches of steel in his breast. I felled him with my left hand.

LADY INGER. Ay—the right was too good for such work.

OLAF SKAKTAVL. That is your affair; —the thought was yours. — And now to Sweden! Peace be with you meanwhile! When next we meet at Ostrat, I shall bring another with me.

(Goes out by the furthest door on the right.)

LADY INGER. Blood on my hands. Then it was to come to that! — He begins to be dear-bought now.

(BIORN comes in, with a number of Swedish men-at-arms, by the first door on the right.)

ONE OF THE MEN-AT-ARMS. Pardon me, if you are the lady of the house— —

LADY INGER. Is it Count Sture you seek?

THE MAN-AT-ARMS. The same.

LADY INGER. Then you are on the right scent. The Count has sought refuge with me.

THE MAN-AT-ARMS. Refuge? Pardon, my noble lady, —you have no power to harbour him; for— —

LADY INGER. That the Count himself has doubtless understood; and therefore he has—ay, look for yourselves—therefore he has taken his own life.

THE MAN-AT-ARMS. His own life!

LADY INGER. Look for yourselves. You will find the corpse within there. And since he already stands before another judge, it is my prayer that he may be borne hence with all the honour that beseems his noble birth. —Biorn, you know my own coffin has stood ready this many a year in the secret chamber. (To the Men- at-Arms.) I pray that in it you will bear Count Sture's body to Sweden.

THE MAN-AT-ARMS. It shall be as you command. (To one of the others.) Haste with these tidings to Jens Bielke. He holds the road with the rest of the troop. We others must in and— —

(One of the Men-at-Arms goes out to the right; the others go with BIORN into the room on the left.)

LADY INGER (moves about for a time in uneasy silence). If Count Sture had not said farewell to the world so hurriedly, within a month he had hung on a gallows, or had sat for all his days in a dungeon. Had he been better served with such a lot? Or else he had bought his life by betraying my child into the hands of my foes. Is it *I*, then, that have slain him? Does not even the wolf defend her cubs? Who dare condemn me for striking my claws into him that would have reft me of my flesh and blood? —It had to be. No mother but would have done even as I. But 'tis no time for idle musings now. I must to work. (Sits down by the table on the left.) I will write to all my friends throughout the land. They rise as one man to support the great cause. A new king, —regent first, and then king— — (Begins to write, but falls into thought, and says softly:) Whom will they choose in the dead man's place? —A king's mother— —? 'Tis a fair word. It has but one blemish—the hateful likeness to another word. —King's *mother* and king's *murderer*. *—King's mother—one that takes a king's life. King's mother—one that gives a king life.

*The words in the original are "Kongemoder" and "Kongemorder, " a difference of one letter only.

(She rises.) Well, then; I will make good what I have taken. —My son shall be king! (She sits down again and begins writing, but pushes the paper away again, and leans back in her chair.) There is no comfort in a house where lies a corpse. 'Tis therefore I feel so strangely. (Turns her head to one side as if speaking to some one.) Not therefore? Why else should it be? (Broodingly.) Is there such a great gulf, then, between openly striking down a foe and slaying one—thus? Knut Alfson had cleft many a brain with his sword; yet was his own as peaceful as a child's. Why then do I ever see this—(makes a motion as though striking with a knife)—this stab in the heart—and the gush of red blood after? (Rings, and goes on speaking while shifting about her papers.) Hereafter I will have none of these ugly sights. I will work both day and night. And in a month—in a month my son will be here— — — —

BIORN (entering). Did you strike the bell, my lady?

LADY INGER (writing). Bring more lights. See to it in future that there are many lights in the room

(BIORN goes out again to the left.)

LADY INGER (after a pause, rises impetuously). No, no, no; —I cannot guide the pen to-night! My head is burning and throbbing— — (Startled, listens.) What is *that?* Ah, they are screwing the lid on the coffin in there. When I was a child they told me the story of Sir Age, * who rose up and walked with his coffin on his back. —If he in there were one night to think of coming with the coffin on his back, to thank me for the loan? (Laughs quietly.) Hm—what have we grown people to do with childish fancies? (Vehemently.) But such stories are hurtful none the less! They give uneasy dreams. When my son is king, they shall be forbidden.

*Pronounce *Oaghe*. [Note: "Age" has a ring above the "A", "Oaghe" an umlaut above the "e". —D. L.]

(Goes up and down once or twice; then opens the window.) How long is it, commonly, ere a body begins to rot? All the rooms must be aired. 'Tis not wholesome here till that be done.

(BIORN comes in with two lighted branch-candlesticks, which he places on the tables.)

LADY INGER (who has begun on the papers again). It is well. See you forget not what I have said. Many lights on the table! What are they about now in there?

BIORN. They are busy screwing down the coffin-lid.

LADY INGER (writing). Are they screwing it down *tight?*

BIORN. As tight as need be.

LADY INGER. Ay, ay—who can tell how tight it needs to be? Do you see that 'tis well done. (Goes up to him with her hand full of papers, and says mysteriously:) Biorn, you are an old man; but *one* counsel I will give you. Be on your guard against all men—both those that *are* dead and those that are still to die. —Now go in—go in and see to it that they screw the lid down tightly.

BIORN (softly, shaking his head). I cannot make her out.

(Goes back again into the room on the left.)

LADY INGER (begins to seal a letter, but throws it down half-closed; walks up and down awhile, and then says vehemently:) Were I a coward I had never done it—never to all eternity! Were I a coward, I had shrieked to myself: Refrain, ere yet thy soul is utterly lost! (Her eye falls on Sten Sture's picture; she turns to avoid seeing it, and says softly:) He is laughing down at me as though he were alive! Pah! (Turns the picture to the wall without looking at it.) Wherefore did you laugh? Was it because I did evil to your son? But the other, —is not he your son too? And he is *mine* as well; mark that! (Glances stealthily along the row of pictures.) So wild as they are to-night, I have never seen them yet. Their eyes follow me wherever I may go. (Stamps on the floor.) I will not have it! (Begins to turn all the pictures to the wall.) Ay, if it were the Holy Virgin herself— — ——- Thinkest thou *now* is the time——? Why didst thou never hear my prayers, my burning prayers, that I might get back my child? Why? Because the monk of Wittenberg is right. There is no mediator between God and man! (She draws her breath heavily and continues in ever-increasing distraction.) It is well that I know what to think in such things. There was no one to see what was done in there. There is none to bear witness against me. (Suddenly stretches out her hands and whispers:) My son! My beloved child! Come to me! Here I am! Hush! I will tell you something: They hate me up there—beyond the stars— because I bore you into the world. It was meant that I should bear the Lord God's standard over all the land. But I went my own way. It is therefore I have had to suffer so much and so long.

BIORN (comes from the room on the left). My lady, I have to tell you—— Christ save me—what is this?

LADY INGER (has climbed up into the high-seat by the right-hand wall). Hush! Hush! I am the King's mother. They have chosen my son king. The struggle was hard ere it came to this—for 'twas with the Almighty One himself I had to strive.

NILS LYKKE (comes in breathless from the right). He is saved! I have Jens Bielke's promise. Lady Inger, —know that——

LADY INGER. Peace, I say! look how the people swarm. (A funeral hymn is heard from the room within.) There comes the procession. What a throng! All bow themselves before the King's mother. Ay, ay; has she not fought for her son— even till her hands grew red withal? —Where are my daughters? I see them not.

NILS LYKKE. God's blood! —what has befallen here?

LADY INGER. My daughters—my fair daughters! I have none any more. I had *one* left, and her I lost even as she was mounting her bridal bed. (Whispers.) Lucia's corpse lay in it. There was no room for two.

NILS LYKKE. Ah—it has come to this! The Lord's vengeance is upon me.

LADY INGER. Can you see him? Look, look! It is the King. It is Inger Gyldenlove's son! I know him by the crown and by Sten Sture's ring that he wears round his neck. Hark, what a joyful sound! He is coming! Soon will he be in my arms! Ha-ha! —who conquers, God or I.

(The Men-at-Arms come out with the coffin.)

LADY INGER (clutches at her head and shrieks). The corpse! (Whispers.) Pah! It is a hideous dream.

(Sinks back into the high-seat.)

JENS BIELKE (who has come in from the right, stops and cries in astonishment). Dead! Then after all— —

ONE OF THE MEN-AT-ARMS. It was himself— —

JENS BIELKE (with a look at NILS LYKKE). He himself— —?

NILS LYKKE. Hush!

LADY INGER (faintly, coming to herself). Ay, right; now I remember it all.

JENS BIELKE (to the Men-at-Arms). Set down the corpse. It is not Count Sture.

ONE OF THE MEN-AT-ARMS. Your pardon, Captain; —this ring that he wore round his neck— —

NILS LYKKE (seizes his arm). Be still!

LADY INGER (starts up). The ring? The ring? (Rushes up and snatches the ring from him.) Sten Sture's ring! (With a shriek.) Oh, Jesus Christ—my son!

(Throws herself down on the coffin.)

THE MEN-AT-ARMS. Her son?

JENS BIELKE (at the same time). Inger Gyldenlove's son?

NILS LYKKE. So it is.

JENS BIELKE. But why did you not tell me— —?

BIORN (trying to raise her up). Help! help! My lady—what ails you?

LADY INGER (in a faint voice, half raising herself). What ails me? I lack but another coffin, and a grave beside my child.

(Sinks again, senseless on the coffin. NILS LYKKE goes hastily out to the right. General consternation among the rest.)